Science

A REFERENCE FOR STUDENTS AND PARENTS

by Mary Dylewski
illustrated by Andrea Champlin

SCHOLASTIC INC.

New York Toronto London Auckland Sydney
Mexico City New Delhi Hong Kong Buenos Aires

ISBN 0-439-67207-4

12 11 10 9 8 7 6 5 4 3 2 1 4 5 6 7 8 9/0

Printed in the U.S.A. 66

First Scholastic printing, September 2004

Cover and interior pages designed by: Bob Filipowich

Developed and produced by: Shereen Gertel Rutman and Joyce Jaskoll Friedman, WWK Consulting Group, Inc.

NOTE TO PARENTS

Helping children do their homework successfully requires some planning. Study habits and time management are important skills for children to learn. The following tips may give you and your child strategies for doing homework more efficiently. Both you and your child will learn to survive Science homework!

- Have your child do homework immediately after coming home from school. A quick snack is okay, but any other activity should wait until later.
- Make sure your child has a quiet, well-lit place to work.
- Help your child gather the materials necessary for his or her homework. Remember to have enough pencils, paper, and other tools ready.
- Try to schedule after-school activities on days when there is not as much homework.
- Long-term projects take planning. Encourage your child to work on a lengthy project in small sections, rather than tackling it all in one evening.
- Children need encouragement and reassurance. Patience and praise help children become better students.
- Encourage your child to notice how science relates to everyday living. This will help spark your child's interest in and enjoyment of learning.

Wanted—Dead or Alive!

You share this planet with billions of other living things called organisms. An **organism** is anything that has all of the characteristics of life. An organism has an orderly structure. An organism is able to reproduce, which means it can make more living things of its own kind. Organisms also grow and change during their lifetimes and adjust, or adapt, to their environments.

Although you share many characteristics with other organisms, you are in a class of your own! In fact, all living things are classified into groups based on similarities. The earliest system of classification was developed in the 1750s and consisted of two large groups, or **kingdoms**: the animal kingdom and the plant kingdom. As scientists learned more and more about living things, they devised a variety of classification systems having different numbers of kingdoms. Even today there is disagreement about which classification system is best. Some scientists argue that there should be three or four kingdoms, but some believe there should be as many as six kingdoms in a classification system.

THE FIVE-KINGDOM SYSTEM

One of the most widely used classification systems is the five-kingdom system. The moneran, protist, and fungus kingdoms are described in this chapter. The plant and animal kingdoms are described in chapters 2 and 3.

In the five-kingdom system, large groups are broken down into smaller groups, each containing fewer kinds of organisms. Kingdoms are divided into groups called **phyla** (sing. **phylum**). People, dogs, cats, fish, and whales belong to the phylum Chordata, which means each of the organisms in that group has a spinal cord. Phyla are divided into **classes**, which in turn are divided into **orders**. People, dogs, cats, and whales belong to the class called mammals, and people belong to the order called primates.

Orders are divided into **families**. People belong to the hominid family. Families are divided into **genera** (sing. **genus**). Genera are further divided into **species**. Although your friends might call you Juan, Min, or Ben, among scientists you and other organisms are known by genus and species names. People belong to the genus **Homo** and the species **sapiens**, which means "man the wise." Your scientific name, then, is ***Homo sapiens***.

MONERANS

The moneran kingdom is made up of bacteria, which are some of the smallest and simplest living things. Bacteria are unicellular (made of only one cell). A **cell** is the smallest living organism. It is also a microscopic building block consisting of different parts that do different things. Bacteria are classified by the shape of their cells: spheres, rods, or spirals.

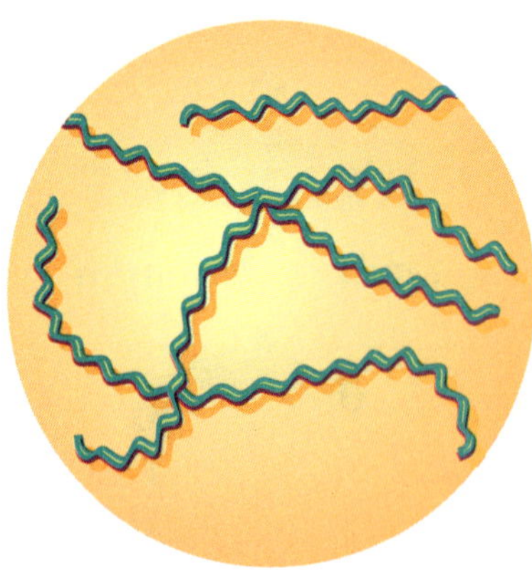

spiral-shaped bacteria

Some types of bacteria can cause diseases, such as tuberculosis, strep throat, ear infections, and tetanus. In contrast, other bacteria can be quite useful to people. Cheese, pickles, and yogurt are only a few of the foods that depend on bacteria for their production. Bacteria are also responsible for the decay of organic material. **Blue-green bacteria**, also known as **cyanobacteria**, can make their own food and are common in ponds, streams, and moist patches of land. Other types of bacteria are parasites, which means these organisms get their energy from other living things.

PROTISTS

The protist kingdom is comprised of more than two hundred thousand species. Scientists classify protists into three groups.

THREE GROUPS OF PROTISTS (PROTOZOANS)

1. Animal-like Protists:
   amoebas, flagellates, ciliates, sporozoans
2. Funguslike Protists:
   slime molds, water molds
3. Plantlike Protists:
   euglenas, diatoms, dinoflagellates, green algae, red algae, brown algae

Viruses are tiny particles that cause many different diseases, from colds and flu to AIDS (Acquired Immunodeficiency Syndrome). Viruses change and reproduce, but they don't grow or move. Are they alive? Write your answer on paper.

PROTISTS

Examples of **animal-like** protists are amoebas, flagellates, ciliates, and sporozoans.

- **Amoebas**, which look like blobs, are protists that constantly change shape. They move by forming **pseudopods** (fingerlike extensions). Most amoebas live in oceans; some live in ponds and streams. Although most amoebas are harmless, a few types can cause disease, such as dysentery.
- **Flagellates** are protists that move by using **flagella**, or whiplike projections. Flagellates can live in fresh or salt waters. Some flagellates live in the digestive tracts of insects and help them digest food. One such flagellate causes the disease known as African sleeping sickness, which is common in tropical areas of Africa.
- **Ciliates** move by beating **cilia**, which are short, hairlike structures that surround the body. Ciliates live in all kinds of bodies of water. A paramecium is a common, slipper-shaped ciliate.
- **Sporozoans** are parasites. These protists cannot move. One type of sporozoan causes malaria.

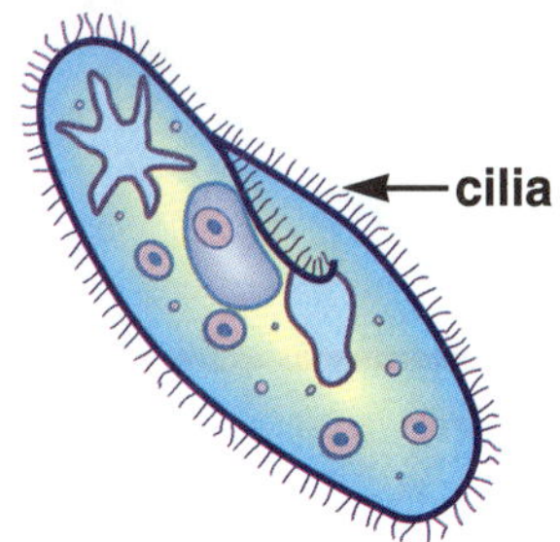

paramecium

Slime molds and water molds are types of **funguslike** protists.

- **Slime molds** can be almost any color. They live in cool, moist, shady places, such as rotting leaves and tree trunks. These protists can move around; they get their food by engulfing it, much as an amoeba does.
- Most **water molds** are white, fuzzy masses. Like their name implies, water molds live in water or in moist places. Some water molds feed on dead organisms; some are parasites.

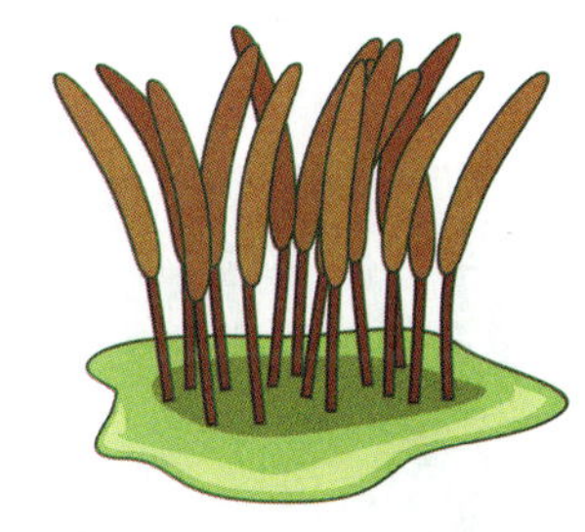
slime mold

Euglenas, diatoms, dinoflagellates, and algae are types of **plantlike** protists.

- **Euglenas** are one-celled protists that live in water. Euglenas are plantlike because they can make their own food. These organisms move with flagella.
- **Diatoms** are one-celled protists that have hard shells. Diatoms live in fresh or salt waters. Diatom shells are used in the production of some toothpastes and paints.
- **Dinoflagellates** are one-celled protists having two flagella. Like diatoms, dinoflagellates can live in fresh or salt waters. One form of this organism is responsible for so-called red tides often associated with the climate phenomenon known as **El Niño**. A red tide occurs when dinoflagellates, which take oxygen from the water, greatly increase in number. When this happens, many fish and other organisms die because they cannot get sufficient oxygen.

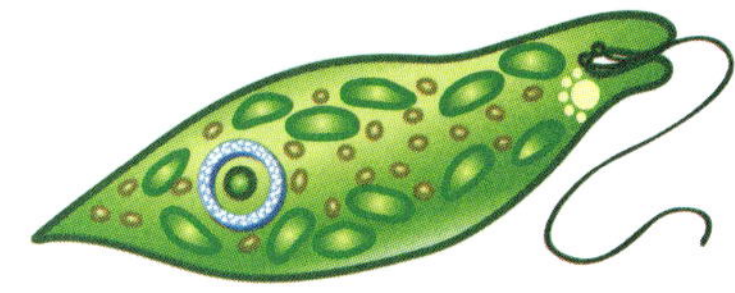
euglena

What are all flagella, cilia, and pseudopods used for? Write your answer on paper.

- **Green algae** are green or yellowish-green in color. Green algae live in fresh water, in oceans, in wet soil, and on tree trunks. Green algae can make their own food. The species of green algae that lives in water moves with flagella.
- **Red algae** are multicellular (made up of many cells). These algae can make their own food and live only in oceans. People use some species of red algae as food.
- Most species of **brown algae** live in cold ocean waters close to shore. These algae anchor themselves to rocks or to the ocean floor. Kelp are a type of brown algae that can be twenty feet (6.1m) long!

FUNGI

The term *fungi* is the plural form of fungus.

Within the fungus kingdom, there are many kinds of fungus among us! Scientists estimate that more than one hundred thousand species of fungi exist. Fungi can grow in many places. One-celled fungi (yeast) can be used to make bread. Some people like many-celled fungi (mushrooms) on their pizzas. And whether you're an athlete or not, you can get athlete's foot—which is an itchy growth of fungus between your toes or on your feet!

Name a medicine that is produced by a type of fungus. Write your answer on paper.

As with bacteria and protists, some fungi are harmful. Fungi can cause foods to spoil, and some mushrooms are poisonous. Dutch elm disease is a fungus that kills hundreds of trees each year. Many fungi, however, serve a very constructive purpose. Fungi can be **decomposers**, which means that they break down decaying wastes and dead organisms.

SOME FUNGUS AMONG US!

What?	Where?
Black mold	Bread
Blue-green, red, brown molds	Fruit peels, dairy products
Yeast	Bread, wine, and beer
Club fungi	Pizza, soups
Asexual fungi	Penicillin, blue cheese

Firmly Planted in the Ground!

PLANTS

PARTS OF A PLANT CELL

Cell wall: protective outer covering of the cell

Cell membrane: flexible sheath that controls movement of materials into and out of the cell

Cytoplasm: clear, thick fluid that surrounds most cell parts

Nucleus: cell part containing the genetic information that controls cell activities and allows information to be passed to successive generations

Ribosome: cell part that makes proteins

Endoplasmic Reticulum: folded cell parts that form a transport system in the cytoplasm

Mitochondria: cell parts that break down food molecules to release energy

Vacuole: cell part that stores food, wastes, or other cell materials

Chloroplast: cell part that uses light energy to convert water and carbon dioxide into simple sugars

Kingdom Plantae (plant kingdom) contains plants such as ferns, mosses, daisies, and pines. Like all organisms, plants are made of cells. You can learn about animal cells in chapter 3.

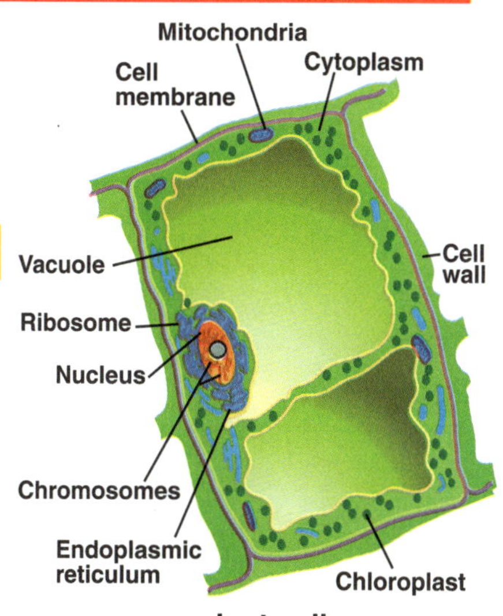

plant cell

PARTS OF PLANTS

Land plants—like organisms in all kingdoms—vary immensely, from leafless ferns to prickly cacti to towering sequoias. Most land plants, however, have three basic parts—leaves, a stem, and roots.

Leaves are broad, flat plant parts that trap light in order to make food for the plant. During **photosynthesis**, a leaf uses a green substance called **chlorophyll** and light energy to change carbon

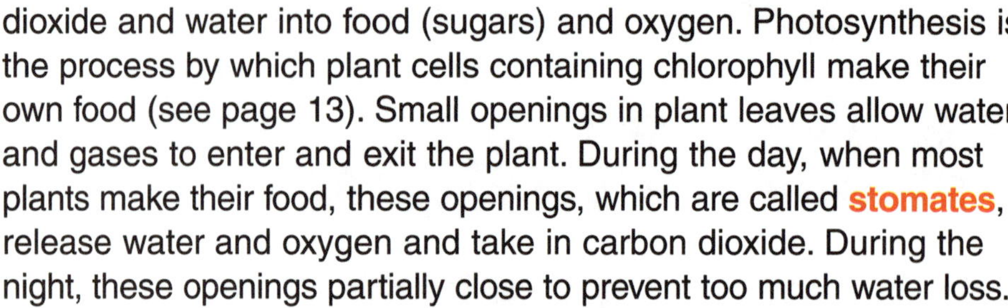

dioxide and water into food (sugars) and oxygen. Photosynthesis is the process by which plant cells containing chlorophyll make their own food (see page 13). Small openings in plant leaves allow water and gases to enter and exit the plant. During the day, when most plants make their food, these openings, which are called **stomates**, release water and oxygen and take in carbon dioxide. During the night, these openings partially close to prevent too much water loss.

The **stem** of a plant has two functions. First, it supports the plant as it grows. Second, a stem helps to transport food, water, and other substances from one part of the plant to another. Some stems also serve as storage places for food. Green stems contain chlorophyll and thus take part in photosynthesis.

Roots have many functions. They anchor plants to the soil. They absorb water and other nutrients from the soil. Roots then transport these substances to the stem, which carries them to the leaves. Some roots, like those of sweet potatoes, store starch.

Some plant roots are edible! Can you name at least three roots that you eat? Write your answer on paper.

FLOWERS

Some plants have complex structures called **flowers**. Flowers that contain petals, sepals, stamens, and pistils are **complete flowers**. Flowers that lack one or more of these major organs are **incomplete flowers**

Petals are the brightly colored flower parts at the top of the stem. Some contain perfume or nectar to attract **pollinators**, such as insects and birds. **Sepals** are green, leaflike structures that protect the flower bud from insects and keep it from drying out. **Stamens** are the male reproductive structures of a flower. The stamen has two parts: the **filament** and the **anther**. The filament is a long, thin stalk. The anther is a large tip at the end of the filament that makes and holds pollen. Pollen grains produce the male reproductive cells, called **sperm** cells. The **pistil** is the female reproductive structure of a flower and has three parts: the **stigma**, the **style**, and the **ovary**. The stigma at the top of the pistil is a sticky structure on which pollen grains land. The style connects the stigma to the ovary. The female reproductive cells, called **egg** cells, are produced in the **ovules** located inside the ovaries.

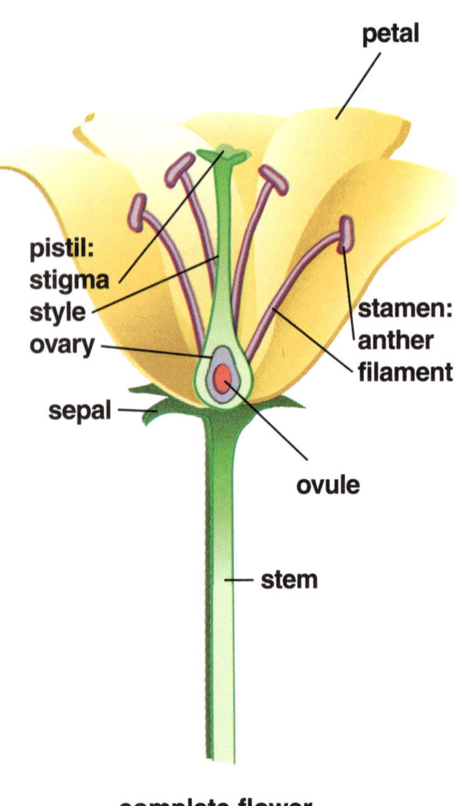

complete flower

Seeds are fertilized ovules. Once fertilization has taken place, a seed begins to develop. The wall of the ovule becomes the hard **seed coat**, which protects the interior parts of the seed. After a seed is fully developed, it may stop growing for a while. When conditions are favorable for growth, a seed begins to germinate. **Germination** is the development of a plant **embryo** into a young plant.

When the eggs in an ovule of a flower are fertilized, the petals, stamens, and parts of the pistil die. **Fruits** then develop from a plant's ovaries. In science, anything that contains a seed or seeds is called a fruit. Fruits can be dry or fleshy. Dry fruits include pecans, almonds, cashews, and other nuts, as well as rice, wheat, and other grains. Fleshy fruits are juicy and include grapes, apples, peaches, watermelons, and many vegetables.

On paper list two fruits that you might find in a dinner salad. Are lettuce and carrots fruits?

KINDS OF PLANTS

There are more than 280,000 species of plants! Scientists classify plants into two groups: non-seed plants and seed plants.

Mosses, ferns, and liverworts are **non-seed plants** that reproduce with spores instead of seeds. A **spore** is a small reproductive cell that can survive even in very harsh environments. When the spores are released from a plant, the wind picks them up or they fall to the ground. A spore germinates to form a small, heart-shaped plant called a gametophyte that contains eggs and sperm. When the eggs are fertilized by the sperm, a new plant called a sporophyte develops. The **fronds** of a fern, for example, grow from a sporophyte.

Mosses and liverworts live in cool, moist environments and they grow close to the ground. Ferns are found in many kinds of **habitats**—places where living things grow—such as tropical forests, coastal evergreen forest floors, stream banks, rocky cliffs, the cold Arctic, and grassy pastures.

There are two types of **seed plants**: conifers and flowering plants. **Conifers** are **gymnosperms**—seed plants in which the seeds are not protected by a fruit. Most conifers are **evergreens**, which means they keep their leaves and stay green all year round. All conifers have needleshaped or scalelike leaves, none produce flowers, and many have cones.

Male and female cones form on different branches of an adult conifer. The male cone produces pollen grains that are carried by the wind to the female cones. Seeds form inside the female cones. When the female cones open, the seeds are released. They germinate to form seedlings, which eventually grow into new trees.

The coal that we now use as fuel began forming more than 300 million years ago. It formed gradually from decaying ferns and other related plants that lived in swampy areas around the world.

Douglas fir

SOME FUN FACTS ABOUT CONIFERS

Conifer	Fun Facts
Douglas firs	Such trees are important to the U.S. lumber industry. These firs can reach heights of 300 feet (91 m).
Pacific yews	Yews don't have cones. One species produces a cancer-fighting drug called taxol.
Giant sequoias	One of the largest of these trees measures more than 272 feet (83 m) tall and 101.5 feet (31 m) around. It weighs almost 6,200 tons (5,642 metric tons).
Bristlecone pines	These are the oldest trees on Earth; one bristlecone pine is more than 4,000 years old!

Flowering plants (angiosperms) develop seeds surrounded by a fruit. Flowering plants are classified into two groups: **monocots** and **dicots**

MONOCOTS	DICOTS
One cotyledon (seed leaf)	Two cotyledons (seed leaves)
Slender leaves with parallel veins	Broad leaves with branched veins
Petals and sepals in multiples of three	Petals and sepals in multiples of four or five
Food-carrying tissue **(phloem)** and water-carrying tissue **(xylem)** are scattered.	Xylem forms a star-shaped mass in the center of the the stem. Phloem is nestled around the xylem.
Include orchids, grasses, corn, and palms	Include tomatoes, roses, oaks, and apples

There are two types of **reproduction** in plants: sexual and asexual.

Plants that reproduce sexually have male and female reproductive organs. Fertilization takes place during a process called **pollination**, in which pollen is transferred to the ovule. Pollination of flowering plants is carried out mainly by insects. Wind is the primary agent for pollination of most grasses and trees. After pollination occurs, sperm cells produced by the pollen join with egg cells in the plant's ovule. This process is called **fertilization**. After fertilization occurs, the ovules develop into seeds.

In the vegetative propagation type of **asexual reproduction**, small pieces of the plant break off and form new plants. The new plant has only one parent and is just like it.

An **annual** is a plant that grows, reproduces, and dies within one growing season. Spinach, beans, sweet peas, zinnias, and poppies are examples of annual plants. Most annuals have **herbaceous** stems that are soft and green.

A **biennial** is a plant that produces leaves and food during its first year, then reproduces and dies the following year. Carrots, cabbage, parsley, and beets are biennial plants.

A **perennial** is a plant that lives from one growing season to another. Trees and plants with **woody** stems (stems that are hard and rigid) are perennials. Other perennials include chives, lavender, lemon grass, oregano, rosemary, and thyme. Tulips, irises, and peonies are also perennials.

Tree rings are made of dead xylem cells. They can be used to tell the age of a tree and the climate conditions in which they grew. Each ring represents one year. Thicker rings show normal or above-average rainfall.

PROCESSES OF PLANTS

On page 10 you learned that photosynthesis is the process by which plant cells containing chlorophyll make their own food. The equation below shows how this process occurs:

$$\underset{\text{(carbon dioxide)}}{6CO_2} + \underset{\text{(water)}}{6H_2O} + \text{light energy} \xrightarrow{\text{chlorophyll}} \underset{\text{(sugar)}}{C_6H_{12}O_6} + \underset{\text{(oxygen)}}{6O_2}$$

During photosynthesis, a plant uses carbon dioxide, water, and light energy to produce sugar and oxygen. The light energy is trapped by the chlorophyll and used to split the water molecules into hydrogen and oxygen. The hydrogen molecule combines with carbon dioxide to make glucose, a simple sugar, which is the plant's food. The oxygen is released into the air.

Transpiration is a process in which water evaporates from a plant's leaves. Plants lose up to ninety percent of their water through transpiration. In fact, a mature apple tree can lose up to four gallons (15 l) of water per hour on a hot, sunny day!

Respiration is a process by which cells release energy from food

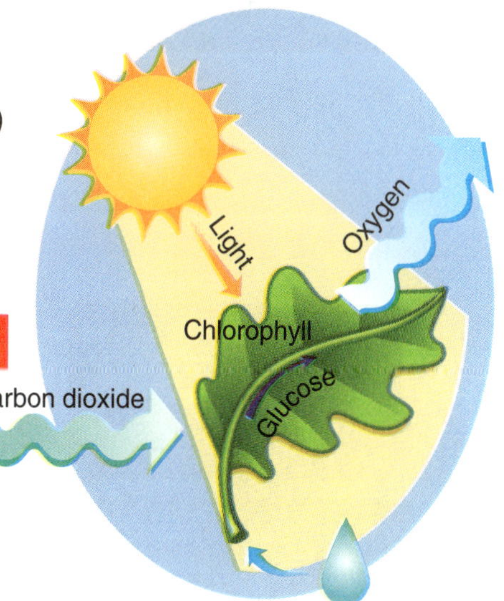

Photosynthesis

molecules to carry out their life activities. Respiration takes place in the cells of all living things. The equation below shows what happens during respiration:

$$\underset{\text{(sugar)}}{C_6H_{12}O_6} + \underset{\text{(oxygen)}}{6O_2} \longrightarrow \underset{\text{(carbon dioxide)}}{6CO_2} + \underset{\text{(water)}}{6H_2O} + \text{heat energy}$$

As you can see, respiration is the reverse of photosynthesis. In respiration, chemical reactions between sugar and oxygen produce carbon dioxide and water. Energy is released in the form of heat as a result of this reaction.

> *Compare the processes of respiration and photosynthesis. How are they the same and how are they different? Write your answers on paper.*

FOOD CHAINS

A **food chain** is a pathway of food and energy. Plants and other organisms that contain chlorophyll can make their own food and, therefore, are called **producers**. They form the first link in a food chain. Organisms that eat other organisms are called **consumers** and they form successive links in a food chain. A consumer that eats producers is a **primary consumer**. Consumers that eat primary consumers are called **secondary consumers**.

A food chain commonly seen in forests is

> *Explain how humans can be either primary or secondary consumers. Write your answer on paper.*

Acorns are the seeds of plants and thus are producers. Mice, which eat plants, are primary consumers in this food chain. Owls, which eat mice and other small animals, are secondary consumers. **Food webs** are made of many interconnected food chains.

CHAPTER 3

Animal, Vegetable, or Mineral?

ANIMALS

Scientists estimate that there are more than four million species of animals on this planet! They are part of what scientists classify as the **animal kingdom**. Like all living things, animals are made of cells. The cell shown on the right is a typical animal cell.

PARTS OF AN ANIMAL CELL

Cell membrane: flexible sheath that controls movement of materials into and out of the cell

Cytoplasm: clear, thick fluid that surrounds most cell parts

Nucleus: cell part containing genetic information that controls cell activities and allows information to be passed to successive generations

Ribosome: cell part that makes proteins

Endoplasmic reticulum: folded cell parts that form a transport system in the cytoplasm

Mitochondria: cell parts that break down food molecules to release energy

Vacuole: cell part that stores food, wastes, or other cell materials

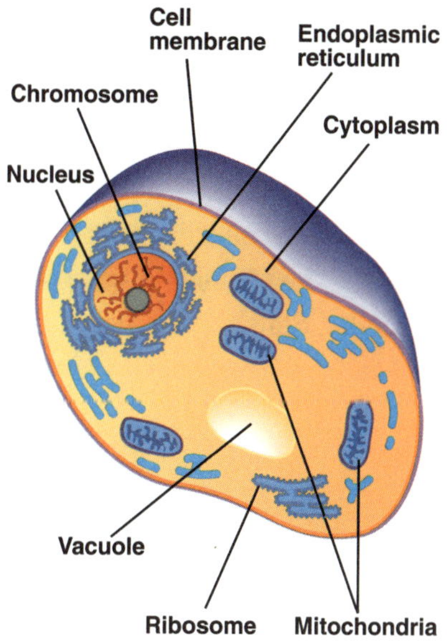

Cell membrane
Endoplasmic reticulum
Chromosome
Cytoplasm
Nucleus
Vacuole
Ribosome
Mitochondria

animal cell

The **nucleus** is the control center of a cell. The nucleus of every living cell contains **nucleic acids** that control the activities of the cell. **DNA** (deoxyribonucleic acid) is a nucleic acid that stores all of the information needed for a cell to function. **RNA** (ribonucleic acid) carries instructions from the DNA for the production of proteins. **Chromosomes** are threadlike structures in the nucleus made up of DNA and proteins. These structures are made of a series of **genes** that carry the "code" that controls the cell's activity and determines the characteristics of the organism.

Look at the plant cell on page 9. What two structures of plant cells are not found in animal cells? Write your answer on paper.

ANIMALS REPRODUCTION OF ANIMALS

New cells are added to plants and animals as they grow and when old cells wear out or are damaged. These new cells form by **cell division**, the process by which a cell splits to create two new cells.

Animals and plants are made up of body cells and sex cells. New body cells are formed by a process of cell division called **mitosis**. There are several stages of mitosis. In the first phase, called prophase, the membrane surrounding the nucleus disappears. Then each chromosome in the cell forms an identical strand.

The second phase of mitosis is metaphase. During this phase, chromosomes line up and become attached to long fibers that run through the cell. Then, during anaphase, the strands of the chromosomes separate and are pulled to opposite sides of the cell by the long fibers. The last phase of mitosis is called telophase. At this point in the cell division, two identical groups of chromosomes exist and the nuclear membrane re-forms around each group. During telophase, the cytoplasm splits to form two cells that each contain a nucleus with exact copies of the original chromosomes.

Cloning is a process whereby a group of genetically identical cells or organisms is produced from a single individual. Bacteria are commonly cloned by drug manufacturers to produce certain drugs. Larger organisms have also been cloned. In 1996, a sheep named Dolly was cloned by a Scottish scientist. Two cloned calves were born the following year in the United States.

Sex cells, or **gametes**, are formed by a process of cell division called **meiosis**. There are two stages of cell division during meiosis. During the prophase stage of the first division, the chromosomes duplicate and similar ones become paired. During the metaphase stage, the pairs of chromosomes become attached to long fibers and are drawn to opposite ends of the cell, which eventually splits to form two cells during anaphase.

During the second division, chromosomes become attached to fibers during metaphase. The chromosome strands separate during anaphase and are pulled to opposite ends of two cells. These two cells divide during telophase to form four new sex cells. Each of these new cells has half the number of chromosomes found in all the other cells in the organism.

REPRODUCTION OF ANIMALS

Some animals only reproduce asexually; other animals reproduce only sexually. Certain animals are able to reproduce either sexually or asexually.

Like plants, animals reproduce in two ways. **Asexual reproduction** is the production of offspring from only one parent cell. Many simple animals reproduce asexually. **Sexual reproduction** is the production of offspring when two different cells combine.

Regeneration is a form of asexual reproduction in which an animal can regrow body parts it has lost. For example, if a planarian (a type of flatworm) is cut into two, the piece with the head will grow a new tail, and the tail piece will grow a new head! Some simple animals, such as certain sponges and hydras, can reproduce asexually through a process called **budding**. In this process, fragments of tissue break off from the parent and form new animals.

REPRODUCTION OF ANIMALS

As with plants, the cells involved in sexual reproduction in animals are called gametes. Fertilization occurs when a male gamete (sperm) combines with a female gamete (egg) to form a single cell. **Internal fertilization** occurs inside the female's body. Internal fertilization occurs in most mammals, reptiles, and birds. **External fertilization** occurs outside the female's body. Most fish and amphibians reproduce this way.

Birds, fish, amphibians, and reptiles lay eggs. Most mammals give birth to live offspring. Some animals produce eggs that hatch before the animal is fully developed, such as a platypus. Some animals develop through a process called **metamorphosis**. Metamorphosis is a series of stages that some organisms go through during their lives. During complete metamorphosis, there are four stages of development: the egg, the larva, the pupa, and the adult. Butterflies, moths, ants, and bees are a few animals that go through complete metamorphosis.

During incomplete metamorphosis, an animal goes through three phases: the egg, the nymph, and the adult. Termites, cockroaches, and grasshoppers are a few insects that go through incomplete metamorphosis.

The table below shows some of the ways animal offspring develop before and after birth.

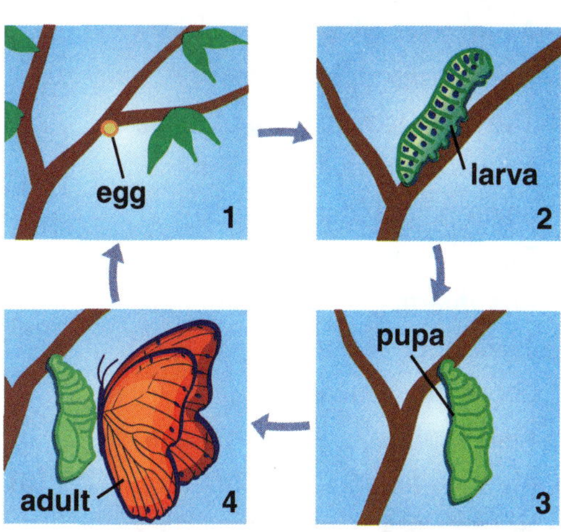

metamorphosis of a butterfly

ANIMAL DEVELOPMENT

Animal	How It Develops
Frogs and toads	Females lay eggs in water, where they are fertilized. Tadpole grows from each egg and develops into an adult frog or toad through metamorphosis.
Butterflies	Females lay eggs on leaves; caterpillar grows from each egg; caterpillar metamorphoses into pupa (or chrysalis), then adult butterfly.
Birds	Females lay eggs with hard shells; female birds **incubate** or keep eggs warm by sitting on them; baby bird develops inside each egg and hatches when it is fully developed.
Kangaroos	Develop partially inside female; at birth, baby crawls into mother's pouch, where it stays until fully developed.
Platypuses	Females lay eggs in nests; eggs hatch to produce animals that aren't fully developed; females take care of young until they are completely developed.

TYPES OF INVERTEBRATES

Animals can be divided into two major groups—invertebrates and vertebrates. The majority of animals on Earth are **invertebrates**, animals without backbones and internal skeletons. Jellyfish, worms, snails, spiders, lobsters, and flies are just a few invertebrates. **Vertebrates** are animals with backbones and internal skeletons. Dogs, frogs, cats, snakes, birds, fish, and people are among the vertebrates that live on this planet.

All invertebrates are *ectotherms*, or cold-blooded. The body temperature of these animals changes to suit the environment they are in. Birds and mammals are *endotherms*, or warm-blooded. Their body temperature stays about the same all the time. Fish, reptiles, and amphibians are cold-blooded vertebrates.

TYPES OF INVERTEBRATES

Sponges are the simplest animals. They have no tissues or organs, and they reproduce both sexually and asexually. Unlike most other animals, adult sponges cannot move from place to place. Sponges live on the bottoms of shallow seas. These animals have many pores. Sponges feed on small organisms in the water that flows through the pores of the sponge.

Cnidarians are animals with stinging cells. Cnidarians have distinct tissues and can reproduce both sexually and asexually. They live in fresh and salt waters and include jellyfish, coral, hydras, and anemones. The most lethal cnidarian is the Australian box jellyfish.

Flatworms include planarians, tapeworms, and flukes. There are about 14,500 species of flatworms. Most flatworms have flat bodies and no body cavities, and they can reproduce sexually or asexually. These animals have only one body opening through which food enters and wastes leave the body. Flatworms live in soil, in fresh and salt waters, and in the intestines of other animals.

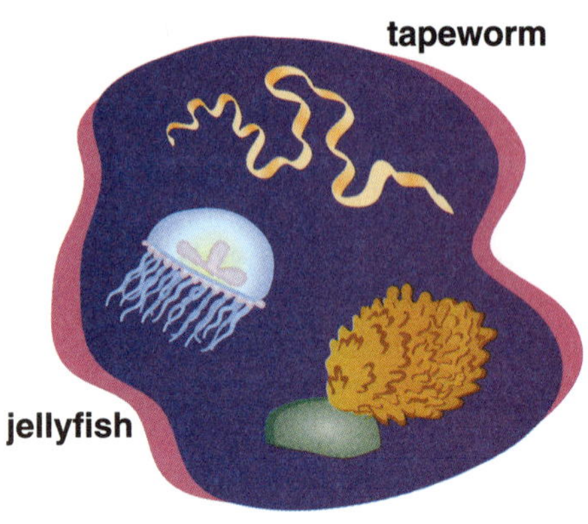

Roundworms have two body openings that make up a simple digestive system. Roundworms are tapered at both ends. Roundworms live in soil and in fresh and salt water; many of them are parasites. In most species of roundworms, separate males and females exist. Some species have both male and female reproductive organs on the same individual.

Earthworms, leeches, and bristleworms are **segmented worms**. Segmented worms are complex invertebrates that have a digestive system, a nervous system, and a closed circulatory system. These worms live everywhere except in deserts and polar regions. A few species of segmented worms reproduce asexually. Some species have both male and female reproductive organs on the same worm. Most segmented worms, however, reproduce sexually.

Octopuses, slugs, and squid are mollusks without shells. The giant squid is the largest invertebrate. When its tentacles are extended, it can measure 59 feet (18 m) long!

Clams, mussels, squid, slugs, snails, and octopuses are **mollusks**. Most mollusks live in the oceans, but some live in fresh water or on land. They have two body openings, a muscular foot used for movement, and a mantle—a thin membrane that covers the internal organs. Some mollusks have shells, and most reproduce sexually.

There are more than one million species of **arthropods**, a group that includes crabs, shrimp, lobsters, spiders, ticks, insects, and scorpions. Most arthropods reproduce sexually. All arthropods have an **exoskeleton**, which is a hard outer covering that protects the animal. Exoskeletons can't grow, so every once in a while, arthropods must **molt**, or shed this outer covering. All arthropods have jointed body parts called **appendages**, which are used for sensing things, swimming, walking, feeding, or mating.

Starfish, sea urchins, sand dollars, and sea cucumbers are **echinoderms**. Reproduction in enchinoderms is either sexual or asexual. All echinoderms have hard, bumpy **endoskeletons**, or internal skeletons that are covered with spines. These animals also have simple nervous and digestive systems. Some echinoderms are **carnivores** (meat-eaters) and eat worms and mollusks. Other echinoderms are **herbivores** (plant-eaters) and feed on algae. Still other echinoderms feed on dead and decaying matter. Echinoderms move with tiny tube feet that have suction cups at their tips. Some echinoderms also use their spines to help them move. All echinoderms live in salt water. The longest echinoderm is the sea cucumber, which can reach 24 inches (61 cm) in length. The largest echinoderm is the sea urchin; some measure almost 7.5 inches (19 cm) in diameter.

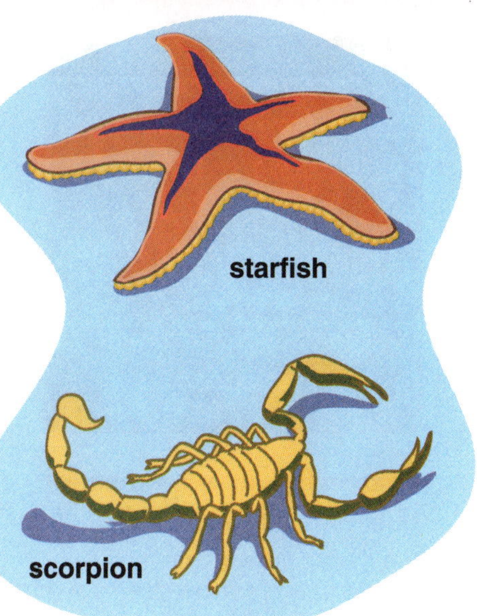

TYPES OF VERTEBRATES

There are more than 20,000 species of **fish**. These species belong to three groups: the lampreys and hagfishes; the sharks and rays; and the bony fish. Fish are aquatic vertebrates with endoskeletons and complex nervous, digestive, and circulatory systems. Most fish reproduce sexually—some lay eggs; others give birth to live young.

Lampreys and hagfishes have a skeleton of cartilage and gills, but they have no paired pectoral or pelvic fins, jaws, or scales. Sharks and rays have a skeleton of cartilage, paired fins, jaws, gills, scales, and highly developed sense organs. Bony fish, which include tuna, sea horses, trout, and eels, have bony skeletons, paired fins, jaws, gills, scales, and highly developed sense organs. The smallest fish, the dwarf goby, is less than an inch (2.5 cm) long. The largest fish, the whale shark, can reach 40 feet (12 m) in length.

Salamanders, newts, frogs, and toads are **amphibians**. An amphibian has lungs; a heart with three chambers; and thin, moist skin. Because amphibian eggs lack shells, reproduction takes place in water. Almost all amphibians go through metamorphosis to reach adulthood. Although they start life in water, most adult amphibians live primarily on land. The largest amphibian is the Japanese giant salamander, which can grow to 5 feet (1.5m) long.

All vertebrates have endoskeletons, but they differ in composition. Lamprey, ray, and shark skeletons are composed of cartilage. The endoskeletons of other vertebrates are made of bone.

TYPES OF VERTEBRATES

Crocodiles are large, four-legged, lizardlike animals. What category of vertebrates do they belong to? Write your answer on paper.

Bats—the only mammals that have wings—are active during the night. They use high-pitched sounds to find food and navigate in the dark. During the day, bats sleep while hanging upside down from tree branches, rafters, and cave roofs.

The smallest amphibian is a frog that measures a mere $\frac{1}{4}$ inch (.64 cm) in length.

Snakes, turtles, alligators, and lizards are **reptiles**. Reptiles have dry, scaly skin; well developed lungs; and with the exception of snakes, four legs with clawed toes. Most reptiles have a heart with three chambers, live in warm regions of the earth, and lay eggs that are fertilized inside the female's body. Most turtles and tortoises are herbivores. Lizards are generally **insectivores**, or insect-eaters. Snakes, crocodiles, and alligators are carnivores.

Birds are unique among animals in that they have feathers, which provide insulation and enable most birds to fly. Birds have wings, hollow bones, a beak, and a four-chambered heart. By observing the shape of a bird's beak, you can guess what the animal eats. A hummingbird's long, slender beak can easily get nectar from a flower. A pelican's beak is used like a net to catch fish. The small, short beak of a goldfinch is used to crack seeds. Because birds don't have teeth, many of them swallow small rocks. The rocks are stored in a saclike organ and help the bird grind up and digest its food. The largest bird is the ostrich; the smallest is the bee hummingbird.

All **mammals** have several things in common. They have hair or fur that helps keep them warm and sweat glands that help keep them cool. Female mammals produce milk, which can be used to feed their young. Many mammals take care of their young until they become adults. Mammals have numerous complex body systems, including a circulatory system with a four-chambered heart. Mammals can be classified in three groups depending on how they reproduce.

MAMMAL DEVELOPEMENT

Types of Mammals	How It Reproduces	Examples
Placental	Carries young inside uterus	humans, dogs, whales
Marsupial	Develops in two stages: First–in mother's body Second–in mother's pouch	Tasmanian devil, koala, kangaroo
Egg-laying	Lays eggs in nest	duck-billed platypus, spiny anteater

From Taiga to Tundra & In-Between: Biomes

A **biome** is an area having a distinct climate, a dominant plant type, and organisms that are **adapted** (suited) to living in that area. There are two kinds of **aquatic biomes**: freshwater and saltwater. **Land biomes** include tundra, taiga, deciduous forests, grasslands, deserts, and tropical rain forests. The map on page 22 shows the general locations of Earth's land biomes.

TYPES OF BIOMES

SALTWATER

Climate: variable

Dominant Plants: red, green, and brown algae; phytoplankton

Common Animals: whales, fish, jellyfish, dolphins, lobsters

FRESHWATER

Climate: variable

Dominant Plants: green algae, cyanobacteria, water lilies, cattails

Common Animals: bony fish, frogs, snakes, birds, alligators, turtles

TUNDRA

Climate: cold and dry

Dominant Plants: some grasses, mosses, lichen

Common Animals: polar bears, musk oxen, arctic foxes, snowy owls

TAIGA

Climate: long cold winters, short mild summers

Dominant Plants: larches, lichen, spruces, pines, firs

Common Animals: caribou, moose, bears, foxes, lynx, birds

TYPES OF BIOMES

DECIDUOUS FORESTS

Climate: four distinct seasons

Dominant Plants: maples, oaks, beeches, sycamores, birches, hickories, perennial wildflowers

Common Animals: black bears, deer, squirrels, salamanders, birds, snakes

GRASSLANDS

Climate: hot and often dry

Dominant Plants: grasses (including oats, rye, and wheat), wildflowers

Common Animals: snakes, bison, lions, antelope, prairie dogs

DESERTS

Climate: very dry, but can be hot or cold

Dominant Plants: cacti, mesquites, sagebrushes, creosotes

Common Animals: scorpions, lizards, mice, camels, coyotes

TROPICAL RAIN FORESTS

Climate: warm and very wet

Dominant Plants: ferns, orchids, vines, palms, evergreen trees

Common Animals: snakes, gorillas, monkeys, leopards, jaguars, anteaters, frogs, ants, birds, bats, sloths, butterflies

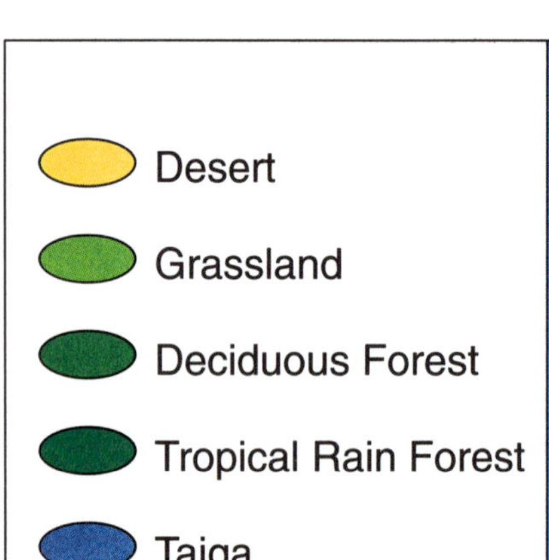

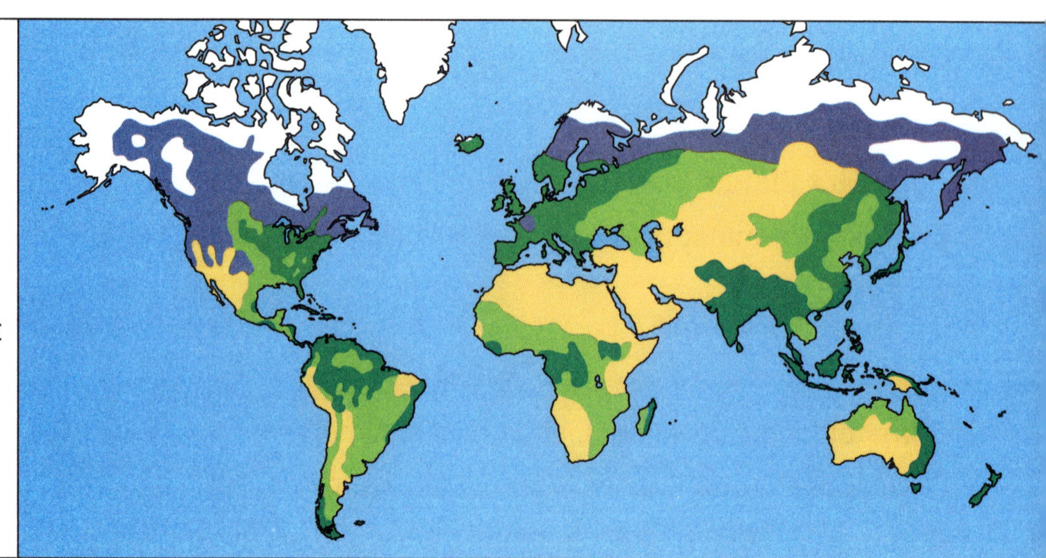

CHAPTER 5

Hard as a Rock!

MINERALS

PROPERTIES OF MINERALS

MINERALS

A word can have different meanings in different situations. Take the word *mineral,* for example. To a life scientist, a mineral is an important element or compound needed by organisms to carry out certain life processes. To an earth scientist, a **mineral** is a substance that meets certain requirements, such as those listed on the right.

FIVE REQUIREMENTS FOR A SUBSTANCE TO BE A MINERAL

- It is a solid.
- It formed as a result of natural processes.
- It is inorganic (nonliving) and was not made by any living things.
- It has a definite internal structure, which means its atoms are arranged in a specific way.
- It has a definite chemical composition, or makeup.

PROPERTIES OF MINERALS

There are more than 2,500 minerals. To distinguish one mineral from another, we look for certain physical characteristics, or **properties**.

Luster refers to the way in which a mineral reflects light. **Metallic** minerals, such as gold, silver, and pyrite, are shiny. **Nonmetallic** minerals can be dull, chalky, pearly, silky, greasy, brilliant, or glassy. Talc, for example, has a pearly luster. Some kinds of quartz are glassy; others are greasy looking. Malachite is a deep green mineral with a silky luster. Diamonds have a brilliant luster.

Color is very useful for identification of some minerals. Malachite is always green. Azurite is always blue. Color is less useful, however, for identifying other minerals, such as quartz. This mineral can occur in a variety of colors: yellow, pink, white, brown, or violet. It can even be colorless.

Cleavage and **fracture** are terms used to describe the way in which a mineral breaks. Minerals that display cleavage tend to break along smooth surfaces. Mica is a mineral that cleaves into thin sheets. Halite, or rock salt, cleaves to produce perfect cubes. Minerals that do not show cleavage are said to fracture, which is breakage that produces rough, uneven, or ragged surfaces. Quartz and copper are two minerals that fracture.

Streak is the color of a mineral when it is finely powdered. Streak is determined by rubbing a mineral on a piece of unglazed white porcelain. Some minerals are the same color as their streaks. But other minerals change quite dramatically. One form of hematite, for example, appears metallic and silvery but leaves a dull, reddish-brown mark when rubbed on unglazed porcelain.

PROPERTIES OF MINERALS

Specific gravity is another property of minerals that can be used for identification. Specific gravity is the weight of a mineral compared with the weight of an equal volume of water. For example, diamond, a nonmetallic mineral, has a specific gravity of 3.5. This means that diamond weighs 3.5 times as much as an equal volume of water. In general, metallic minerals have high specific gravity values. Copper, a metallic mineral, has a specific gravity of 8.9. Platinum, another metallic mineral, has a specific gravity that varies from 14 to 19.

Hardness is the resistance of a mineral to being scratched. Common items, such as a fingernail, a copper penny, and window glass, are used to test hardness, which makes this one of the most useful properties for mineral identification. Friedrich Mohs, a German mineralogist, developed a scale to determine hardness. The scale consists of ten minerals arranged from 1 (softest) to 10 (hardest).

Some minerals have unique characteristics and are thus easy to identify. For example, magnetite is magnetic. Opal scatters light rays to produce a milky or pearly appearance. Fluorite glows, or fluoresces, when exposed to black light. The ability to conduct electricity is a property found in all metals, such as copper, iron, gold, and silver.

MOHS SCALE OF MINERAL HARDNESS

Mineral	Hardness
talc	1
gypsum	2
calcite	3
fluorite	4
apatite	5
feldspar	6
quartz	7
topaz	8
corundum	9
diamond	10

SOME COMMON MINERALS AND THEIR PROPERTIES

Mineral	Hardness	Luster	Color(s)	Breakage	Use(s)
Quartz	7	varies	varies	fractures	optical lenses
Graphite	1.5	metallic	black, steel-gray	cleaves	pencil "lead"
Talc	1	pearly	gray-white, pale green	cleaves	cosmetics, paints, paper, ceramics, talcum powder
Gold	2.5	metallic	golden yellow	fractures	jewelry, money, dentistry
Calcite	3	glassy	white	cleaves	cement
Diamond	10	brilliant	colorless	cleaves	jewelry, abrasives
Halite	2.5	glassy	white	cleaves	table salt, roadway de-icers
Magnetite	6	metallic	black	fractures	magnets

ROCKS

Rocks are earth materials made of one or more minerals. Some rocks, like coal, consist of materials that were once living. Rocks are classified according to the way in which they form.

Igneous rocks form when hot, molten earth materials cool and harden. Some igneous rocks form from **lava**, which is molten material at the earth's surface. Other igneous rocks form from **magma**—molten material that cools deep within the earth. Granite, basalt, obsidian, and pumice are a few examples of igneous rocks.

Most **sedimentary rocks** form when bits or fragments of earth materials, called **sediments**, are pressed or cemented together by earth processes. Some sedimentary rocks form when minerals that are dissolved in ground water are left behind after the water evaporates. Other sedimentary rocks form when wind loses energy and deposits pieces of sand and other earth materials. Some sedimentary rocks form when sediments in the ocean become compacted and cemented together. Sandstone, coal, and some forms of limestone such as chalk are common sedimentary rocks.

Metamorphic rocks are rocks that form from existing rocks. There are three ways in which rocks can become metamorphosed. Rocks can change when they are subjected to the intense heat associated with volcanoes or with bodies of magma. Rocks can also become metamorphic when they are subjected to intense pressures from overlying rocks and sediments. Finally, rocks can become metamorphosed when hot, mineral-rich waters come into contact with the rocks. Heat and solutions often change the chemical makeup of the rocks. Pressure most often changes the texture of the rock. Gneiss, marble, slate, and schist are examples of metamorphic rocks.

THE ROCK CYCLE

Rocks at and beneath the earth's surface are constantly undergoing change. Wind, water, and extreme temperatures can break rocks into smaller pieces, or sediments, and move the pieces from place to place. The breaking down of rocks into sediments is called **weathering**. Weathering and the transporting, or moving around, of sediments is called **erosion**.

As sediments accumulate, those at the bottom are pressed together by the weight of the sediments above. This process is called **compaction**. The natural process of gluing sediments together is **cementation**. Compaction and cementation are important processes in the formation of sedimentary and igneous rocks.

ROCKS
THE ROCK CYCLE

Which mineral could you use to pick up metal paper clips that have spilled on the floor? Which mineral might you use to complete your homework? Write your answers on paper.

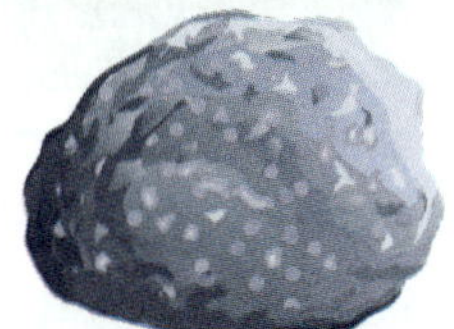
igneous rock (basalt)

sedimentary rock (coal)

metamorphic rock (schist)

Name two examples of each kind of rock. Write your answer on paper.

THE ROCK CYCLE
FOSSILS

Heat and pressure at and below the earth's surface can cause metamorphic rocks to form. If there is enough heat and pressure to melt existing rocks, magma forms. The magma then cools, hardens, and becomes sedimentary or igneous rock through a process called **lithification**.

All of the processes—melting, lithification (turning into rock), compaction, cementation, weathering, and erosion—constantly change the earth's rocks. These processes make up a never-ending cycle of changes called the **rock cycle**.

FOSSILS

What kind of animal left the fossils shown in the illustration? Write your answer on paper.

Fossils are the preserved remains or traces of organisms that once lived on Earth. Most fossils are embedded in sedimentary rocks. But there are other ways in which fossils are preserved.

- **Frozen in ice** In the past, our planet was much colder than it is today. During these cold spells, large portions of Earth were covered with masses of ice called glaciers. At times, animals and prehistoric people became trapped in this ice. Entire bodies of a few woolly mammoths have been preserved this way.
- **Trapped in amber** Hardened tree sap is known as amber. In the past, insects have been trapped in this sticky sap while it was still a liquid. When the sap hardened to amber, the insects' entire bodies were preserved.
- **Trapped in tar** Pools of tar, a very sticky substance, sometimes form at the earth's surface. Between 10,000 and 40,000 years ago, many plants and animals became trapped in tar pits in what is now Rancho La Brea in California. Thousands of bones and teeth of saber-toothed cats have been found in these tar pits.
- **Petrifaction** Petrifaction is the process by which an object is turned to stone, or **petrified**. Many fossils have been formed when the buried remains of plants or animals have been replaced, little by little, by minerals dissolved in ground water, while retaining the form of the original remains. These petrified remains are as hard as rock—in fact, they are rock!
- **Molds and casts** Sometimes organisms become trapped in mud and sand. Over time, the mud and sand become rock. Water moving through the rock can dissolve the original organic material, leaving behind an imprint of the organism. This imprint, or cavity, is called a fossil **mold**. If the mold becomes filled with sediments that harden, a fossil **cast** is formed.
- **Traces** Tracks and other evidence of animal activity preserved in the earth's rocks are called **trace fossils**. Footprints, burrows, and holes are common trace fossils.

Tree trunks in the Petrified Forest in Arizona are petrified fossils. Many fossilized bones, shells, and teeth are also petrified remains.

CHAPTER 6

One If by Land, Two If by Sea

Earth is often called the Blue Planet because nearly three-fourths (140 million square miles or 364 million sq. km) of its surface is covered with water! Most of this water is in the oceans. The fresh water used for cooking, drinking, bathing, and watering lawns makes up only a very small portion of the earth's total amount of water.

BODIES OF WATER

The **ocean** covers more than 71 percent of the earth's surface. Although this water is actually one big ocean having interconnected bodies of water, it is commonly thought of as four major separate oceans. These are the Pacific Ocean, the Atlantic Ocean, the Indian Ocean, and the Arctic Ocean. The Pacific Ocean is the largest and deepest body of salt water. It makes up about 46 percent of the world ocean. Its deepest point is the Mariana Trench, which extends 36,412 feet (11,098 m) below the ocean's surface!

A **lake** is a body of water surrounded by land. The water that fills most lakes comes from melting snow and ice, underground springs, rivers, runoff from the land, and falling rain or snow. Most lakes are freshwater bodies. However, the Great Salt Lake in northern Utah is, as its name implies, a saltwater lake. Lake Superior is the largest freshwater lake. It covers roughly 31,815 square miles (82,719 sq. km)! The largest saltwater lake is the Caspian Sea, which is 143,630 square miles (372,000 sq. km).

A **river** (also known as a stream or a creek) is a body of fresh water that flows within a channel called a **rill**. The point where a river forms is its **source**; the point where it ends is its **mouth**. The sides of the channel are known as the **banks** of the river. The longest river is the Nile River, which is 4,145 miles (6,671 km) long. The Nile empties into the Mediterranean Sea. The Amazon River in South America is about 4,000 miles (6,440 km) long. Asia's longest river is the Yangtze, which measures about 3,915 miles (6,300 km) in length. The longest river in North America is the Mississippi at 2,348 miles (3,779 km). Europe's longest river is the Volga River, which is 2,194 miles (3,531 km) in length.

EARTH'S WATER SUPPLY

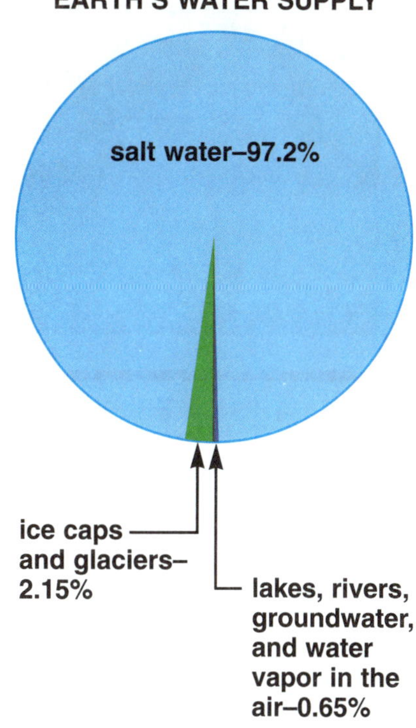

BODIES OF WATER LANDFORMS

As a river flows from its source to its mouth, it erodes and deposits vast amounts of sediments. Erosion, or the weathering and picking up of sediments, occurs in areas where the water flows fast. **Deposition**, the dropping of sediments, occurs in areas where the river slows down. The processes of erosion and deposition happen in areas where the river curves, or **meanders**. Erosion occurs along the outside of a meander. Deposition occurs on the inside of a meander. A **tributary** is a smaller river or stream that flows into a larger one.

Glaciers are large masses of ice moving slowly across the earth's surface. Alpine glaciers are ice masses that form in mountain valleys. Continental glaciers are ice sheets that cover a large area of a landmass. Glaciers are responsible for enormous amounts of erosion.

Earth's **water cycle** is the continuous movement of water from the surface of oceans, rivers, and lakes into the air, from the air to the land, and from the land back to the oceans, rivers, and lakes. The transformation of liquid water into a gas is called **evaporation**. **Precipitation**—in the form of rain, snow, sleet, or hail—forms when gases condense to form a liquid or a solid. **Runoff** is precipitation that flows across the surface of the land. Precipitation that seeps into the ground becomes **groundwater**.

EARTH'S WATER CYCLE

1. Water falls to the earth as rain.
2. Water collects in lakes, rivers, and oceans.
3. As the sun warms the water, it evaporates.
4. Water vapor in the air cools and condenses into tiny droplets, forming clouds.

LANDFORMS

Rising above the surface of the ocean are pieces of land called **continents**. There are seven continents: North America, South America, Africa, Asia, Europe, Australia, and Antarctica. Each of these landmasses is dotted with features called **landforms**. There are three major landforms: plains, plateaus, and mountains.

Plains are broad, relatively flat areas of land. The Great Central Lowlands of South America, much of central Europe, the deserts of northern Africa, and the Great Plains of eastern Australia are plains. The Great Plains region of the United States lies roughly between the Appalachian Mountains and the Rockies. These flat, dry, grassy plains make up much of the farmland in the country.

Plateaus, like plains, are relatively flat areas of land. Plateaus, however, are elevated higher above sea level than are the plains. Millions of years ago, the land was lifted by forces deep within the earth. Since then, weathering and erosion have helped level out the surfaces, creating plateaus. The Colorado Plateau in the western United States, the Great Central Plateau of Africa, and the Deccan Plateau of India are a few of Earth's more notable plateaus.

Mountains are landforms that rise very high above the surrounding land. Mountains can be classified according to the way in which

they were formed. **Fold mountains** form when forces deep within the earth's crust cause large slabs of rocks to be squeezed from opposite sides. The Appalachian Mountains in the eastern United States, the Alps of Europe, and the Himalayas of Asia are fold mountains. **Dome mountains** form when large masses of rock are pushed upward. The Black Hills in South Dakota and the Adirondacks of New York are dome mountains. **Fault-block mountains** are landforms made of vast blocks of rock that have moved up along a fault line in the earth's crust. The sharp, jagged peaks of the Grand Tetons are typical of fault-block mountains. **Volcanic mountains** form when lava cools and accumulates at the earth's surface. Mount Saint Helens in the state of Washington and Aconcagua in South America are volcanic mountains.

Erosion mountains form from the erosion of sedimentary rock. The Catskill Mountains in New York state are erosion mountains.

fold mountain

dome mountain

fault-block mountain

volcanic mountain

The earth's landmasses don't "end" at the shoreline. The **continental shelf** is the gently sloping part of a continent that extends below the ocean and eventually becomes the ocean floor. The shelf extends from the shore toward the ocean basin. Continental shelves are very narrow along some continental boundaries but extend over 900 miles (1,450 km) seaward along other coasts.

A **continental slope** is a steeply dipping boundary from the outer edge of the continental shelf seaward to the **abyssal plain**, which is the broad, flat region of the deep ocean floor. The continental slope marks the boundary between continental crust and oceanic crust.

WEATHER

Convert 25°C to degrees Fahrenheit. Write your answer on paper.

A weather forecaster reports that the relative humidity is 60 percent. Explain what she means. Write your answer on paper.

WEATHER

Weather is the state of the atmosphere at a given time and place. Weather includes wind speed and direction, air pressure, air temperature, the amount of moisture in the air (humidity), the kind of **precipitation**, or moisture, (if any), and the types of clouds in the sky. Wind speed is measured with an instrument called an **anemometer**. The direction from which the wind is blowing can be determined with a **weather vane**. Air pressure, also called **atmospheric pressure** or **barometric pressure**, is the weight of the air pressing down on the earth's surface. Air pressure is measured with a **barometer**. Air temperature is measured with a **thermometer**. Air temperature is measured on two different scales: the Fahrenheit (F) scale and the Celsius (C) scale. The equations below can be used to convert values on one scale to values on the other scale.

$$\text{Celsius to Fahrenheit} = (^\circ C \times \tfrac{9}{5}) + 32 = {}^\circ F$$

$$\text{Fahrenheit to Celsius} = (^\circ F - 32) \times \tfrac{5}{9} = {}^\circ C$$

Humidity is the amount of water vapor, or moisture, in a volume of air. Water vapor is water in the gaseous phase. Humidity is measured with a **hygrometer**. Humidity depends on air temperature. Warm air can hold more moisture than cool air can. **Relative humidity** is the actual amount of water vapor in the air compared to the total amount of water vapor the air could hold at that temperature. Relative humidity is usually expressed as a percent.

nimbus

Clouds are made from millions of tiny water droplets or bits of ice suspended in the air. **Cirrus clouds** are white, feathery clouds of ice crystals high in the atmosphere. They are associated with fair weather but can indicate an approaching storm. **Cumulus clouds** are thick, puffy masses that resemble pieces of popcorn with flat bottoms. Cumulus clouds often indicate fair weather but can produce precipitation. **Stratus clouds** occur in layers, or sheets, and often cover the entire sky. Stratus clouds usually produce light precipitation. A stratus cloud close to the ground is called fog. **Nimbus clouds**, which usually produce precipitation, are dark gray clouds with puffy edges.

cirrus

cumulus

stratus

Rain, snow, sleet, and hail are forms of precipitation that fall from clouds to the earth. **Rain** is precipitation that falls to the earth as liquid water. Rain occurs when the air temperature is above freezing (0˚C or 32˚F). **Snow** is produced when air temperature in the clouds and at the earth's surface is below freezing. **Sleet** is frozen rain that may start out as snow or rain. If it starts as snow, it changes to rain as it passes through a layer of warm air. This rain then passes through a layer of cold air near the surface and freezes. **Hail** is frozen precipitation that forms during a thunderstorm when tiny pieces of ice are tossed up and down through the thundercloud before falling to the earth's surface.

An **air mass** is a body of air that develops over land or water. An air mass has the same properties as the region over which it developed. Air masses that form over continents are generally dry. Air masses that form over oceans are moist. Air masses that develop over cold land are cool or cold; those that form over warm surfaces are warm or hot.

When two different air masses meet, they form a boundary called a **front**. A **warm front** forms when a warm air mass replaces a cold air mass. A **cold front** develops when a cold air mass invades a warm air mass. **Stationary fronts** form when an air mass stops moving. **Occluded fronts** develop when two cool air masses meet, usually lifting a warm air mass and trapping it between them. Stormy weather is often associated with fronts.

STORMY WEATHER

Storm	Characteristics
Hurricane	Develops over oceans; eye (calm central zone) forms as air sinks; can cause violent winds, heavy rains, flooding
Tornado	Develops over land; funnel-shaped storm with strong, swirling winds; moves in a narrow path; can cause great destruction
Thunderstorm	Develops when warm, moist air masses are forced aloft; brings lots of rain to an area; accompanied by thunder and lightning; the most common storm
Blizzard	Develops in the winter in northern latitudes; brings cold temperatures and significant snowfall; can cause high winds

CLIMATE POLLUTION

The distance of a point on the earth's surface from the equator is called *latitude*. Latitude is the distance measured north and south from the equator to either the North or South Pole. Latitude is measured in degrees. Polar climates occur in areas between $66\frac{1}{2}°$ north and south latitudes and the poles. Tropical climates occur in regions between $23\frac{1}{2}°$ north and south latitudes.

EFFECTS OF ACID RAIN

1. Acid rain forms when sulfur dioxide and other air pollutants from cars and factories mix with moisture in the air.
2. Sulfuric and nitric acids form and fall to the earth's surface with rain or snow.
3. Acid rain damages buildings and other structures made of stone; changes the acidity of lakes, rivers, and other small bodies of water; and often reduces crop yields.

CLIMATE

Climate is the average of all weather conditions of an area over an extended period of time. Climates vary throughout the earth, creating different types of environments. (See the biome map on page 22.) There are five major factors that affect the climate of a region: the circulation of the atmosphere (which produces winds), the surface features of an area (topography), the height of a place above sea level (altitude), the distance of a place from oceans and large lakes, and the distance of a place from the equator (latitude).

Climates can be classified according to the amount of solar energy an area receives. **Polar climates** are always very cold, while **tropical climates** have hot temperatures year round. **Temperate climates** lie between the tropics and the polar regions. Areas with temperate climates generally have cold winters and hot summers.

POLLUTION

Pollution refers to all human activities that have harmed the natural environment. **Smog** is a type of air pollution that forms when sunlight reacts with gases and other substances in the air. Smog can hang over an area for days if air masses are stationary, and it can harm all living things.

The **greenhouse effect** is a process by which the earth's atmosphere traps the heat produced by incoming solar radiation and keeps it close to the surface. Greenhouse gases, mainly carbon dioxide, come from factories, car exhaust, and animals. Cutting down trees and burning fossil fuels such as coal can increase the greenhouse effect, which can lead to global warming.

CHAPTER 7

Once Upon a Time...

The earth is more than 4.6 billion years old! To better understand the earth's long history, scientists have divided its past into segments based on the ages of certain rocks and the appearance and disappearance of various life forms. This calendar of major events is called the **geologic timescale**.

GEOLOGIC TIMESCALE

PRECAMBRIAN EON (4600 MYA to 570 MYA*)

Oxygen-poor atmosphere and oceans form. Simple organisms, such as algae and bacteria, develop in the oceans. Over time, more complex life forms such as protists evolve. Mountains are rising on parts of the land.

PALEOZOIC ERA (570 MYA to 240 MYA)

Cambrian period (570 MYA to 500 MYA): Southern Hemisphere continents join together. Warm oceans cover much of the land. Invertebrates such as trilobites thrive in the warm oceans. The first jawless fish appear.

Ordovician period (500 MYA to 435 MYA): Many mountains, including the Appalachians, continue to form. Volcanoes erupt in western North America. Invertebrates called graptolites and conodonts dominate the oceans.

Silurian period (435 MYA to 410 MYA): Present-day North America and Europe form a single landmass. Caledonian Mountains start to form. Corals and fish with jaws live in the seas. First land plants appear.

Devonian period (410 MYA to 360 MYA): Mountains form in eastern North America. Seas intermittently cover parts of North America. Fish dominate these seas. Amphibians and insects evolve on land. First forests, which include ferns, grow in swampy areas.

Mississippian period (360 MYA to 330 MYA): Appalachian Mountains continue to rise. Glaciers cover much of the earth's landmasses. Complex invertebrates thrive in seas. Winged insects evolve on land.

* MYA means millions of years ago

Pennsylvanian period (330 MYA to 290 MYA): All landmasses form a single supercontinent. Swamps cover much of North America. Reptiles and insects rule the land. Club mosses and seed-bearing ferns flourish. First conifers appear.

Permian period (290 MYA to 240 MYA): Ural Mountains start to rise. Glaciers retreat from much of the land. Reefs form in western North America. Dominant organisms include cone-bearing plants, ferns, fish, amphibians, and reptiles. Many marine invertebrates in the oceans become **extinct**, or no longer exist anywhere on the earth.

MESOZOIC ERA (240 MYA TO 63 MYA)

Triassic period (240 MYA to 205 MYA): Supercontinent begins to fragment. Atlantic and Indian Oceans open. The western Cordillera (Sierra Nevada and Rockies) in North America and the Verkhoyansk Mountains in Russia start to rise. Reptiles flourish. First dinosaurs and mammals appear. Conifers flourish.

Jurassic period (205 MYA to 138 MYA): Mountains in western North America (Sierra Nevada and Rockies) continue to form. Seas cover large areas of land in many parts of the world. Invertebrates dominate these seas. First birds appear. Palms and cone-bearing trees thrive. Largest dinosaurs live on land and in water.

Cretaceous period (138 MYA to 63 MYA): Continents move toward their present-day positions. Many volcanoes are erupting on the earth. Flowering plants appear. Placental mammals evolve. Many living things on land, including dinosaurs, and in the sea become extinct.

CENOZOIC ERA (63 MYA to present)

Tertiary period (63 MYA to 2 MYA): The Alps, Andes, and Himalayas begin to rise. Present-day continents and oceans exist. Horses, primates, and humans evolve. Flowering plants flourish on land.

Quaternary period (2 MYA to present): Ice sheets cover much of North America and Europe, parts of South America and Asia, and all of Antarctica. Many living things become extinct during this Ice Age. Mammals, flowering plants, and insects dominate land.

PLATE TECTONICS

Earth is a dynamic planet. Ocean basins have opened and closed several times. Mountains have formed and have been worn away. Continents have shifted positions many times. These changes are still happening today. The driving force behind most of them is a process called plate tectonics.

PLATE TECTONICS
EARTHQUAKES

The **theory of plate tectonics** states that the earth's crust, or outer layer, and upper mantle are broken into enormous slabs called plates. These plates are in very slow but constant motion. Tectonic plates collide, separate, or move horizontally past one another, creating some of the changes described earlier. The regions where plates are in contact with one another are called **plate boundaries**.

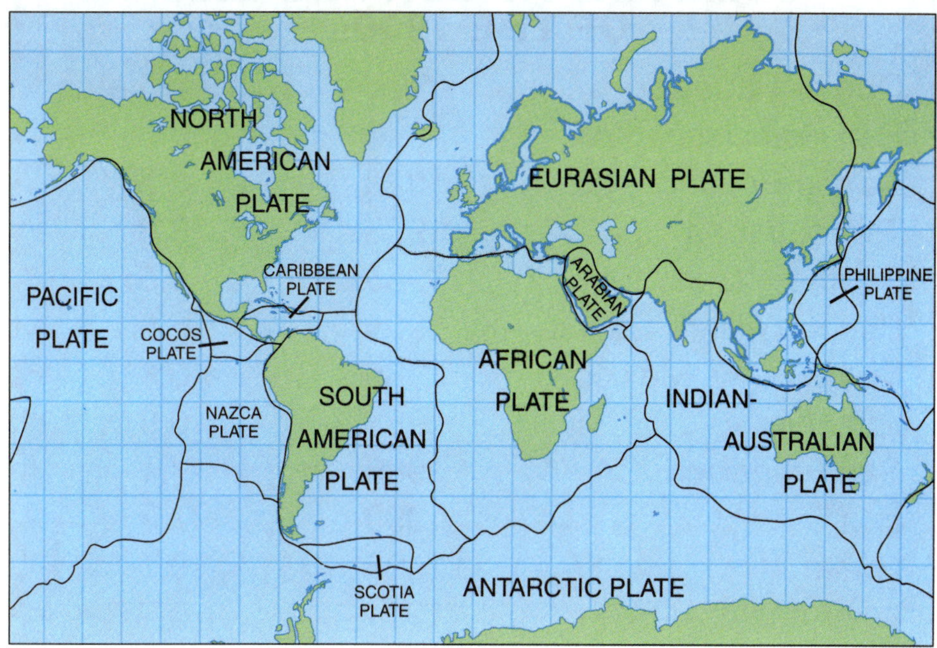

Places where tectonic plates collide are called **convergent plate boundaries**. Fold mountains, some types of volcanoes, and deep-sea trenches form at these plate margins. Earthquakes also occur when tectonic plates collide. Places where tectonic plates separate, or move apart, are called **divergent plate boundaries**. Ocean basins form at these types of plate margins. Tectonic plates move horizontally past one another at **transform fault boundaries**. Earthquakes are common along these types of boundaries. The San Andreas fault in California is a transform fault boundary.

EARTHQUAKES

Earthquakes are vibrations of the ground caused by the sudden movement of rocks. Most earthquakes occur along or near plate boundaries. During an earthquake, tremendous amounts of energy are released. The point within the earth at which this release of energy takes place is called the **focus** of the earthquake. The point on the earth's surface directly above the focus is the **epicenter** of the quake.

The strength of an earthquake, or the energy released, can be measured on the **Richter scale**. Nearly thirty-two times as much energy is released for each increase of 1.0 on this scale.

EARTHQUAKES

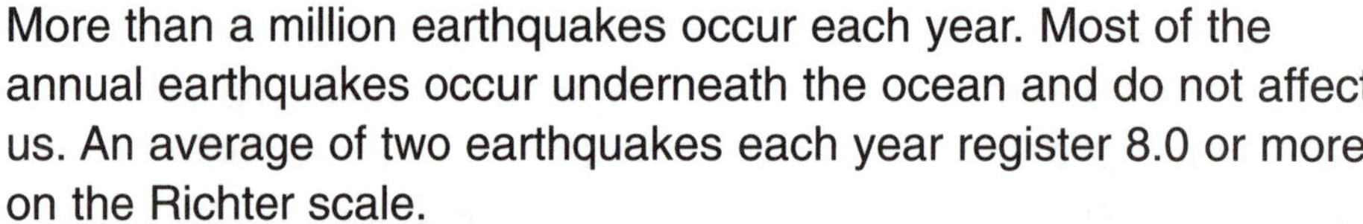

More than a million earthquakes occur each year. Most of the annual earthquakes occur underneath the ocean and do not affect us. An average of two earthquakes each year register 8.0 or more on the Richter scale.

Which tectonic plate includes North America? Write your answer on paper.

SOME MAJOR EARTHQUAKES OF THE 1900s

Quake Location	Year	Richter Value
San Francisco, CA	1906	8.3
Gansu Province, China	1920	8.5
Tokyo, Japan	1923	8.3
Southern Chile	1960	9.5
Prince William Sound, AK	1964	8.5
Mexico City, Mexico	1985	8.1
Armenia	1988	6.9
San Francisco, CA	1989	7.1
Iran	1990	7.7
Guam	1993	8.1
Los Angeles, CA	1994	6.7
Kobe, Japan	1995	7.2

A **seismograph** is an instrument that records earthquake waves. Earthquakes can generate three types of waves. **Primary waves** are the fastest waves. **Secondary waves** are slower than primary waves. **Surface waves** are the slowest earthquake waves, but they cause the most damage. By using a **seismogram**, or record of earthquake waves, scientists can determine the distance from the seismograph recording station to the epicenter of the earthquake.

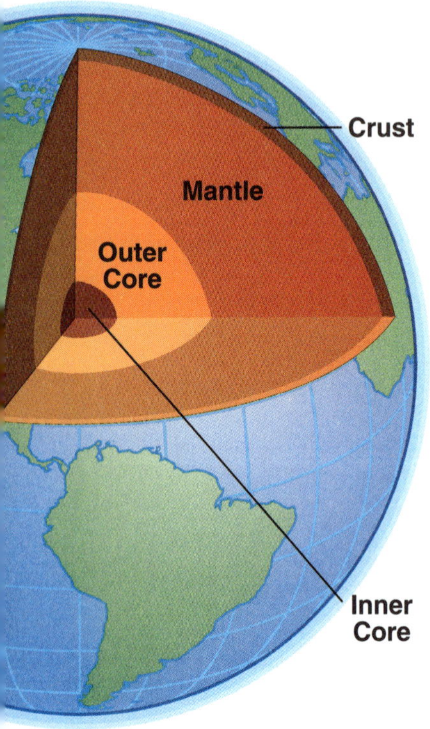

By studying earthquake waves, scientists have identified several distinct layers of the earth. The **crust** is the outer layer. It ranges between 3 and 22 miles (4.8 and 35 km) in thickness. The crust is thickest beneath high mountain ranges and thinnest at the ocean floor. The earth's middle layer, the **mantle**, is about 1,800 miles (2,900 km) thick. The upper part of the mantle is rigid; the lower part is partially melted and behaves like putty. The earth's innermost layer is the **core**, which is made of iron and nickel. The core is divided into two parts: a solid inner core about 760 miles (1,224 km) thick and a liquid outer core about 1,420 miles (2,286 km) thick.

VOLCANOES

A **volcano** is an opening in the earth's crust from which **lava**, or molten rock, flows. Some volcanic eruptions, such as those that occur on the ocean floor, are relatively quiet, meaning that lava flows from the opening and quickly cools to form igneous rock. Volcanic eruptions can also be violent and can result in the formation of mountains if lava or other volcanic debris (ash and cinders) flows from the same opening over an extended period of time. Three types of volcanic mountains are shield volcanoes, cinder cones, and composite cones.

Shield volcanoes are broad, slightly domed mountains with sloping sides. These volcanoes are made of the igneous rock basalt. Basalt is a fine-grained extrusive rock that forms when silica-rich lava cools and changes into rock. When shield volcanoes erupt, the lava flows slowly and "quietly" from several vents in the crust. Volcanoes in the Hawaiian Islands are shield volcanoes. Kilauea, located on the island of Hawaii, is probably the world's most active volcano. Mauna Loa, the largest volcano, is also a shield volcano. Mauna Loa measures more than 5.7 miles (9.2 km) from its base on the ocean floor to its peak on Hawaii! Most shield volcanoes form over hot spots in the earth's mantle.

Cinder cones are explosive volcanoes made of lava fragments. Because this debris is unconsolidated, cinder cones have very steep sides. Cinder cones are relatively small mountains, usually less than 1,000 feet (305 m) high. Paricutín, in Mexico, and Krakatoa, in Indonesia, are cinder cone volcanoes.

On paper list the layers of the earth from the inside out! Then, using an average thickness of 12 miles (19.3 km) for the crust, compute the earth's diameter. The formula for finding the diameter of a circle is 2 times r (radius).

ANATOMY OF A VOLCANO

Term	Meaning
aa (AH ah)	jagged, blocky lava
ash	sand-sized volcanic debris
bombs	large, semi-molten pieces of volcanic debris
caldera	large opening produced when the top of a volcano collapses into the magma chamber
cinders	small volcanic bombs
crater	the depression at the summit of a volcano
magma chamber	underground pool of liquid rock that fuels a volcano
pahoehoe (pah HOH ee hoh ee)	ropy lava that forms smooth sheets of rock
pillow lavas	billowy lava beds deposited underwater
vent	opening in the crust through which lava flows

VOLCANOES

Composite cones are made of alternating layers of volcanic debris and lava. Most composite cones have steep slopes near their summits and gently sloping flanks. Mount Pelée on the Caribbean island of Martinique, Mount Saint Helens in the state of Washington, and Fujiyama in Japan are composite volcanoes. Many composite volcanoes form along convergent plate boundaries.

On paper arrange the following types of volcanic material from largest to smallest: ash, bombs, and cinders.

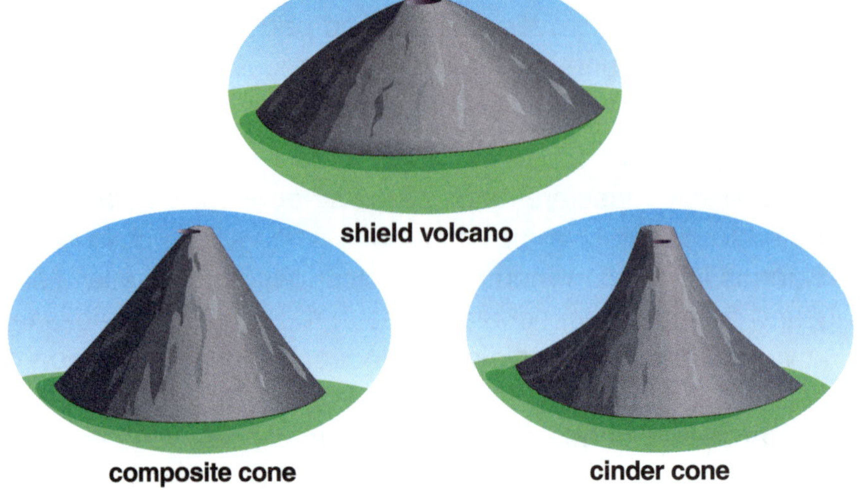

MAJOR VOLCANOES

Year	Volcano	Country	Type of Volcano	Eruptive Force
79	Vesuvius	Italy	composite cone	violent
1669	Mt. Etna	Sicily	composite cone	moderate
1883	Krakatoa	Indonesia	cinder cone	violent
1906	Vesuvius	Italy	composite cone	moderate
1915	Mt. Lassen	United States (California)	composite cone	moderate
1933	Mauna Loa	United States (Hawaii)	shield	quiet
1943	Paricutín	Mexico	cinder cone	moderate
1963	Surtsey	Iceland	shield	moderate
1980	Mt. Saint Helens	United States (Washington)	composite cone	violent
1985	Nevado del Ruiz	Colombia	composite cone	violent
1989	Kilauea Iki	United States (Hawaii)	shield	quiet
1991	Pinatubo	Philippines	composite cone	violent

CHAPTER 8

Out of This World

EARTH'S MOON

The planet Earth has only one natural satellite: the moon, which formed more than 4.5 billion years ago. The moon's surface has mountains, valleys, and plains. Lunar plains (maria) are broad, flat regions made of the igneous rock called basalt. Lunar depressions (craters) form when debris in outer space collides with the moon. Unlike Earth, the moon has no atmosphere, and its gravity is about one-sixth that of Earth.

Earth's moon rotates on its axis once every $29\frac{1}{2}$ days. During this time, the moon revolves once around Earth in relationship to the sun. Because these two motions take the same amount of time, we always see the same side of the moon. The moon's revolution, however, causes **phases**, or changes, in the moon's appearance.

An **eclipse** occurs when one object passes into the shadow of another object. There are two kinds of eclipses. An eclipse of the moon, a **lunar eclipse**, occurs when the full moon is in Earth's shadow. An eclipse of the sun, a **solar eclipse**, occurs when Earth is in the shadow of a new moon. Shadows cast into space by Earth or the moon have two parts. The **umbra** is the dark, cone-shaped inner shadow. The **penumbra** is the lighter shadow surrounding the umbra. A **total eclipse** occurs in a region covered by the umbra. A **partial eclipse** occurs in a region covered by the penumbra.

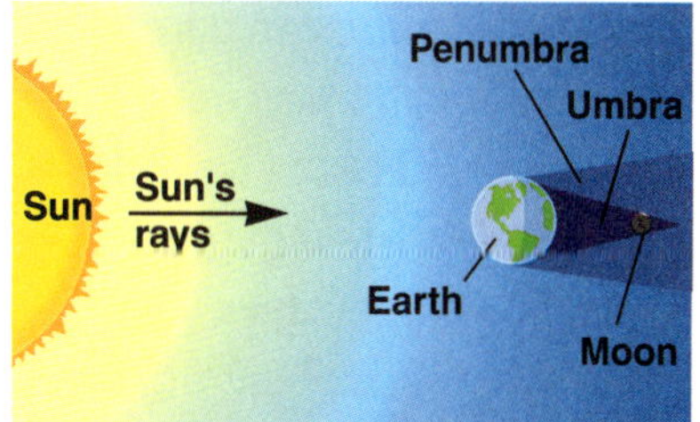

lunar eclipse

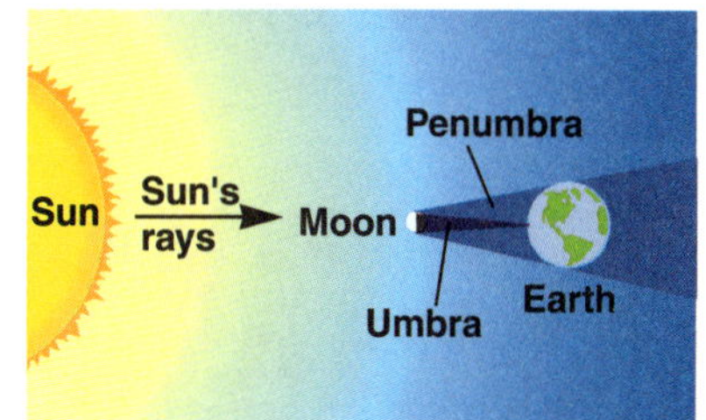

solar eclipse

The United States Apollo space program made it possible for astronauts Neil Armstrong and Edwin Aldrin to be, on July 20, 1969, the first people to walk on Earth's moon. Five additional Apollo flights landed on the moon over the next three years. The Apollo program ended in 1972, but it provided scientists with samples of lunar rocks and other information about Earth's nearest neighbor. Exploration of Earth's moon began again in January 1998, with the launch of the *Lunar Prospector*. This spacecraft, which is in orbit 60 miles (97 km) above the moon's surface, has detected evidence of frozen water on the moon. The existence of water would be invaluable for the future establishment of colonies on the lunar surface.

Gravitational attraction among Earth, its moon, and the sun causes **tides**. Tides are changes in water levels at shorelines around the world. **Spring tides** occur at new moon and full moon phases, when the sun, moon, and Earth line up. The gravitational forces of the three bodies combine to produce the highest high tides and lowest low tides of the month. **Neap tides** occur at the first and third quarter phases, when the moon, Earth, and sun are at right angles. Neap tides have the lowest high tides and the highest low tides of the month.

THE SUN

The sun, which is at the center of our solar system, is a star. **Stars** are tremendously hot, bright spheres of glowing gases. Most of the sun's mass consists of the gases hydrogen and helium. Helium is formed from hydrogen by a process called **fusion**. This is a nuclear reaction that occurs at very high temperatures (about 15 million °C or 27 million °F) and under extreme pressure in the sun's core. Energy from this reaction travels outward from the sun by radiation and convection.

The **photosphere**, or visible surface of the sun, is much cooler than its core. The light that illuminates our solar system is emitted from the sun's photosphere. **Sunspots** are relatively cool, dark areas of the photosphere. Outward from the photosphere is the **chromosphere**, a bright red layer composed mostly of hydrogen. **Prominences** are glowing gases that shoot out from the chromosphere. The outermost layer of the sun is the **corona**, which is visible only during a total solar eclipse.

Never look directly at the sun. Solar radiation can damage your eyes and may cause blindness. Always wear sunscreen when outdoors, even on cloudy days. Ultraviolet (UV) light from the sun can cause skin cancer.

The sun is the star that is closest to Earth. The distance between the sun and Earth is approximately 93 million miles (150 million km). At an estimated age of 5 billion years, our sun is halfway through its life cycle. Its mass is about 2.2×10^{27} metric tons, or 330,000 times more massive than Earth!

Earth revolves around the sun once every $365\frac{1}{4}$ days. At the same time, Earth rotates on its axis once every 24 hours. Earth's axis is tilted about $23\frac{1}{2}°$ from the plane of its orbit (its path) around the sun. This tilt, along with the angle at which the sun's rays strike a given location, causes the seasons.

Earth is closest to the sun in December, when it is winter in the United States. But seasons are not related to Earth's distance from the sun. Changes in season are due to the tilt of the Earth's axis and the angle at which the sun's rays strike a given region.

Which tides—spring or neap—exhibit the greatest difference between high and low tides? Explain your answer on paper.

STARS

A star begins as an enormous cloud of gas and dust called a **nebula**. Over time, gravitational attraction causes the particles to move toward one another. As the nebula contracts, its temperature rises. When the temperature reaches about 2 million ˚F (1.1 million ˚C), fusion begins and a star is born. For millions of years, the star radiates energy out into space.

When the star begins to run out of hydrogen, changes start to take place. The changes depend on the mass of the star. When, for example, the outer layers of a medium-sized star expand, it forms a **giant**. As the star's hydrogen is exhausted, the star contracts to form a **white dwarf**. As the star's helium is exhausted, the star becomes a **black dwarf**.

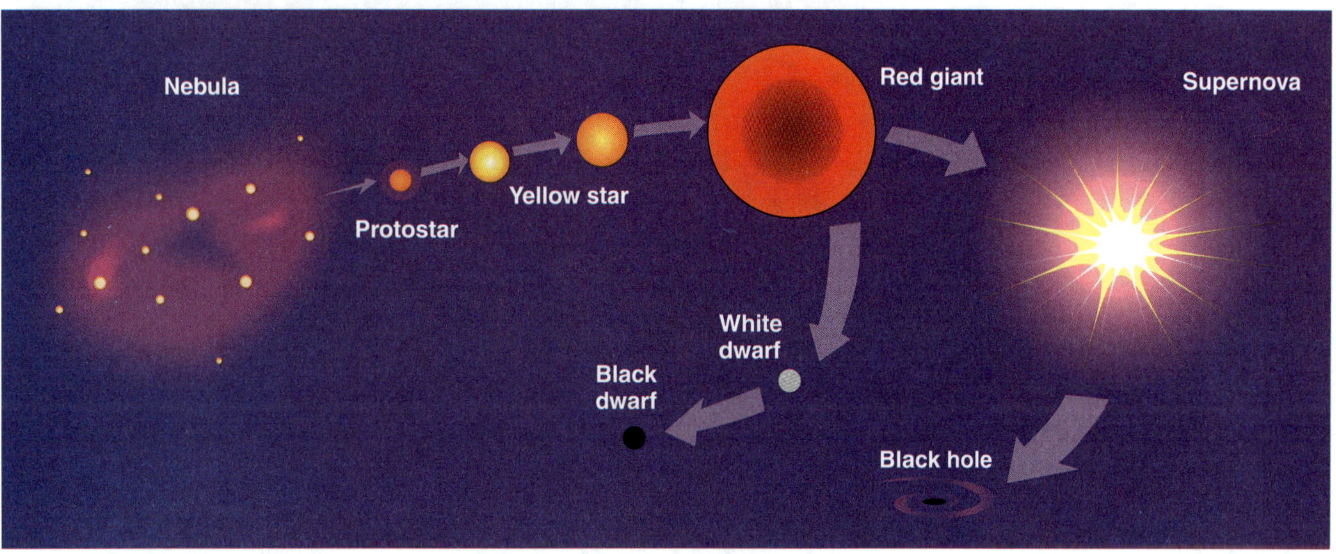

If the star is at least three times more massive than our sun, it expands to form a **supergiant**. When the outer part of a supergiant explodes, a **supernova** occurs. As the core of the supergiant collapses, a **neutron star** forms. If this core is still more than three times more massive than our sun, the star quickly evolves into a black hole. A **black hole** is a star that is so dense that nothing, including light, can escape its gravitational field.

A **constellation** is a group of stars that forms a pattern in the night sky. Although the stars in a constellation appear to be relatively close to one another, they are, in fact, often billions and billions of miles apart. Scientists measure such large distances in space in light-years. A **light-year** is the distance light travels in one year, which is nearly 6 trillion miles (9.7 trillion km)! Some of the most visible constellations in the northern hemisphere are Canis Major, Orion, Ursa Major (Big Dipper), and Ursa Minor (Little Dipper).

STARS

During which month is Earth closest to the sun? Write your answer on paper.

Stars are classified according to brightness and temperature. Ninety percent of the stars we can see fit into a band called the main sequence. Stars with medium-sized diameters, including our sun, are main-sequence stars.

OUR SOLAR SYSTEM

OUR SOLAR SYSTEM

Our **solar system** includes nine planets, their satellites, the sun, and numerous asteroids, comets, and meteoroids. **Asteroids** are pieces of rock that generally orbit the sun between Mars and Jupiter. The largest known asteroid is Ceres, which is more than 600 miles (970 km) in diameter. **Comets** are mixtures of dust, rock, ice, and some frozen gases. Pieces of rock that break off when asteroids collide are called **meteoroids**. A meteoroid that burns up in Earth's atmosphere is a **meteor**, sometimes called a "shooting star." A meteor that strikes Earth is called a **meteorite**.

Mercury
Distance from sun: 36 million miles (58 million km)
Diameter: 3,030 miles (4,878 km)
Orbit (in Earth time): 88 days
Rotation (in Earth time): 59 days
Rings: none
Satellites: none

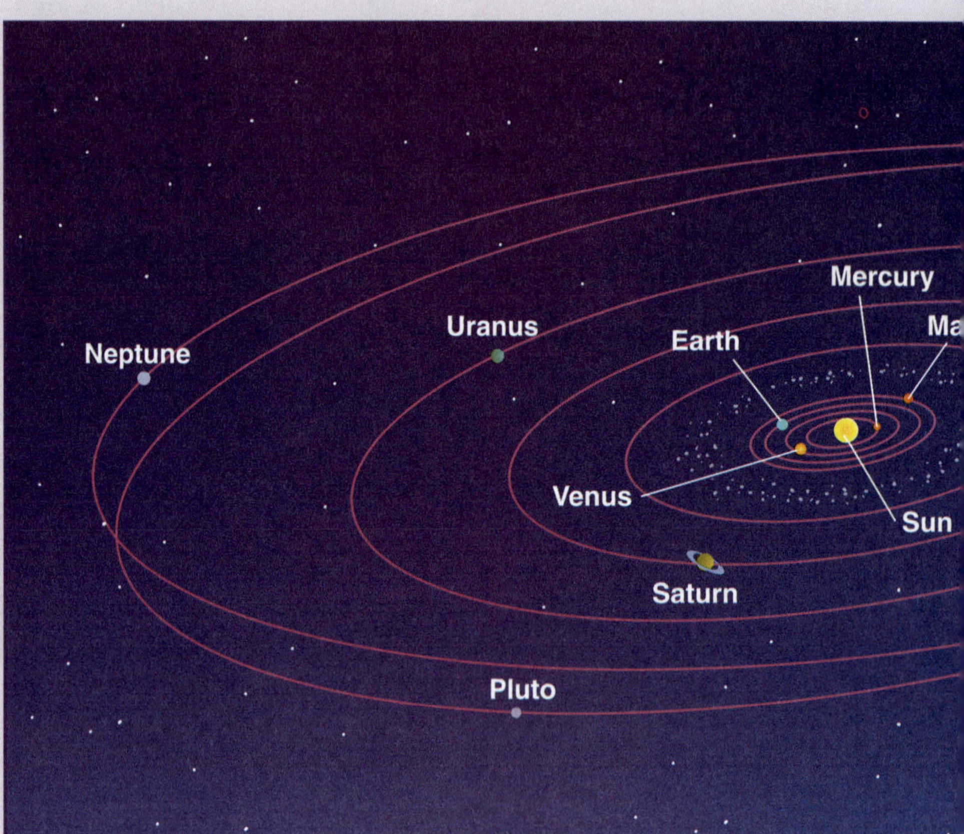

Venus
Distance from sun: 67 million miles (108 million km)
Diameter: 7,520 miles (12,100 km)
Orbit (in Earth time): 225 days
Rotation (in Earth time): 243 days
Rings: none
Satellites: none

Earth
Distance from sun: 93 million miles (150 million km)
Diameter: 7,927 miles (12,762 km)
Orbit (in Earth time): 365 $\frac{1}{4}$ days
Rotation (in Earth time): 23 hours, 56 minutes
Rings: none
Satellites: 1

Mars
Distance from sun: 142 million miles (228 million km)
Diameter: 4,220 miles (6,794 km)
Orbit (in Earth time): 687 days
Rotation (in Earth time): 24.3 hours
Rings: none
Satellites: 2

Jupiter
Distance from sun: 484 million miles (779 million km)
Diameter: 88,730 miles (142,855 km)
Orbit (in Earth time): 11.9 years
Rotation (in Earth time): 9 hours, 55 minutes
Rings: 3
Satellites: 16

OUR SOLAR SYSTEM

Uranus
Distance from sun: 1.787 billion miles (2.877 billion km)
Diameter: 31,570 miles (50,828 km)
Orbit (in Earth time): 84 years
Rotation (in Earth time): 16–28 hours
Rings: 11
Satellites: 17

Neptune
Distance from sun: 2 billion miles (4.5 billion km)
Diameter: 30,200 miles (48,622 km)
Orbit (in Earth time): 165 years
Rotation (in Earth time): 18–20 hours
Rings: 4
Satellites: 8

Saturn
Distance from sun: 888 million miles (1,430 million km)
Diameter: 74,980 miles (120,718 km)
Orbit (in Earth time): 29.5 years
Rotation (in Earth time): $10\frac{1}{2}$ hours
Rings: 7 (thousands of ringlets)
Satellites: 23

Pluto
Distance from sun: 3.67 billion miles (5.9 billion km)
Diameter: 1,460 miles (2,350 km)
Orbit (in Earth time): $248\frac{1}{2}$ years
Rotation (in Earth time): 6 days
Rings: none
Satellites: 1

PLANETARY FUN FACTS

- Mercury's temperature has a tremendous range from day to night. Because Mercury has no atmosphere, it can reach 342°C (648°F) in the day.
- Sulfuric acid in Venus's atmosphere gives the clouds a yellowish color.
- Earth is the only planet known to support life as we recognize it.
- In 1997, the space probe *Pathfinder* sent back 2.6 billion bits of information about the "Red Planet."
- Jupiter's Great Red Spot is actually a violent, whirling storm that was first observed in the late 1600s.
- Saturn is a gaseous planet, the density of which is so low it could float in water!
- Uranus's axis of rotation, unlike the other planets, is tilted on its side!
- One of Neptune's moons, Triton, has a diameter of about 2,000 miles (3,220 km) and an atmosphere of methane.
- The planet Pluto is named for the Roman god of the dead.

GALAXIES

GALAXIES

Our solar system belongs to a group of stars called the Milky Way Galaxy. A **galaxy** is an enormous group of stars, gases, and dust particles held together by gravitational forces. There are three types of galaxies. The Milky Way—about 100,000 light-years in diameter—is a **spiral galaxy** in which arms wind out from a central region. Our sun—only one of an estimated two hundred billion stars in the Milky Way—is located about 30,000 light-years from the galaxy's center. **Elliptical galaxies** are generally shaped like footballs, but some are spherical. **Irregular galaxies**, which are smaller than spiral or elliptical galaxies, have a variety of shapes. The large and small Magellanic Clouds are irregular galaxies.

Most scientists believe that the universe formed between fifteen billion and twenty billion years ago as the result of a tremendous explosion. The **Big Bang Theory** states that all the matter in the universe was initially concentrated into an incredibly dense mass. An explosion, or big bang, propelled this matter in many directions. As the matter cooled, hydrogen and helium began to form. Eventually, the matter began to collect and form galaxies, which are currently moving away from one another. This moving apart of the galaxies indicates that the universe is expanding.

CHAPTER 9

What's the Matter?

MATTER
COMPOSITION OF MATTER

MATTER

Everything around you is made of matter. **Matter** is anything that has mass and takes up space. The three common states, or phases, of matter are solid, liquid, and gas. **Plasma** is a fourth state of matter that exists only at very high temperatures, such as those found in stars. A **solid** is matter that has a definite volume and a definite shape. A **liquid** is matter that has a definite volume, but no particular shape. A liquid takes the shape of the container that holds it. A **gas** is matter that has no definite shape or volume. A gas expands to fill any container it occupies. The volume of a gas is measured according to the pressure containing it. Like a gas, a plasma has no definite shape or volume.

The boiling point of water is 212°F (100°C). Liquid water changes to a gas at this temperature. The freezing point of water is 32°F (0°C). Liquid water changes to a solid at this temperature.

Matter can change state when its temperature changes or when the pressure exerted on it changes. Melting occurs when a solid is heated and changes to a liquid. The change of phase from a liquid to a solid is called freezing. A liquid changes into a gas when the liquid boils and produces steam. A liquid can also change into a gas without boiling by a process called **evaporation**. When a gas cools, it condenses, or changes into a liquid. This process is called **condensation**. Under certain circumstances, matter can change directly from a solid to a gas, or a gas to a solid, without becoming a liquid. This process is called **sublimation**.

Describe some every-day examples of water in changing states. Write your answers on paper.

COMPOSITION OF MATTER

All matter is made up of extremely tiny particles called **atoms**. These atoms are constantly moving. Even the atoms that make up solids are moving. Atoms move fastest in matter that is in the gaseous state and slowest in matter that is in the solid state.

All atoms have similar structures and a dense core called the **nucleus**. The nucleus of all atoms (except hydrogen) contains **protons**, which have positive charges, and **neutrons**, which have no charges. Negatively charged particles called **electrons** orbit the nucleus of an atom. The nucleus of a hydrogen atom consists of a single proton.

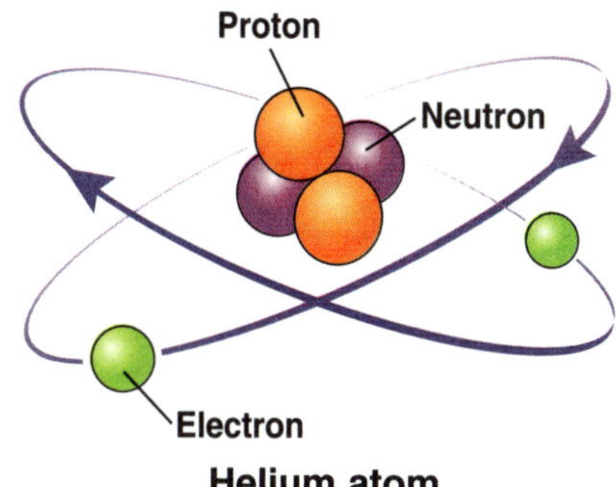

Helium atom

ELEMENTS

ELEMENTS

An **element** is a type of matter that contains only one kind of atom. For example, iron is an element. It contains only iron atoms. Currently, there are 111 known elements. Most of these elements occur naturally; others have been made in laboratories. Elements are arranged in a specific order based on certain properties. This arrangement is called the **periodic table**. The **atomic number** is the number of protons in the nucleus of the atom. Elements are abbreviated by symbols. Elements 57 to 71 are called the Lanthanide series. Elements 89 to 103 are called the Actinide series.

3 **Li** Lithium	4 **Be** Beryllium							
11 **Na** Sodium	12 **Mg** Magnesium							
19 **K** Potassium	20 **Ca** Calcium	21 **Sc** Scandium	22 **Ti** Titanium	23 **V** Vanadium	24 **Cr** Chromium	25 **Mn** Manganese	26 **Fe** Iron	27 **Co** Cobal
37 **Rb** Rubidium	38 **Sr** Strontium	39 **Y** Yttrium	40 **Zr** Zirconium	41 **Nb** Niobium	42 **Mo** Molybdenum	43 **Tc** Technetium	44 **Ru** Ruthenium	45 **Rh** Rhodiu
55 **Cs** Cesium	56 **Ba** Barium	57 to 71	72 **Hf** Hafnium	73 **Ta** Tantalum	74 **W** Tungsten	75 **Re** Rhenium	76 **Os** Osmium	77 **Ir** Iridiu
87 **Fr** Francium	88 **Ra** Radium	89 to 103	104 **Rf** Rutherfordium	105 **Db** Dubnium	106 **Sg** Seaborgium	107 **Bh** Bohrium	108 **Hs** Hassium	109 **Mt** Meitneri

Lanthanide series →	57 **La** Lanthanum	58 **Ce** Cerium	59 **Pr** Praseodymium	60 **Nd** Neodymium	61 **Pm** Promethium	62 **Sm** Samari
Actinide series →	89 **Ac** Actinium	90 **Th** Thorium	91 **Pa** Protactinium	92 **U** Uranium	93 **Np** Neptunium	94 **Pu** Plutoni

ELEMENTS

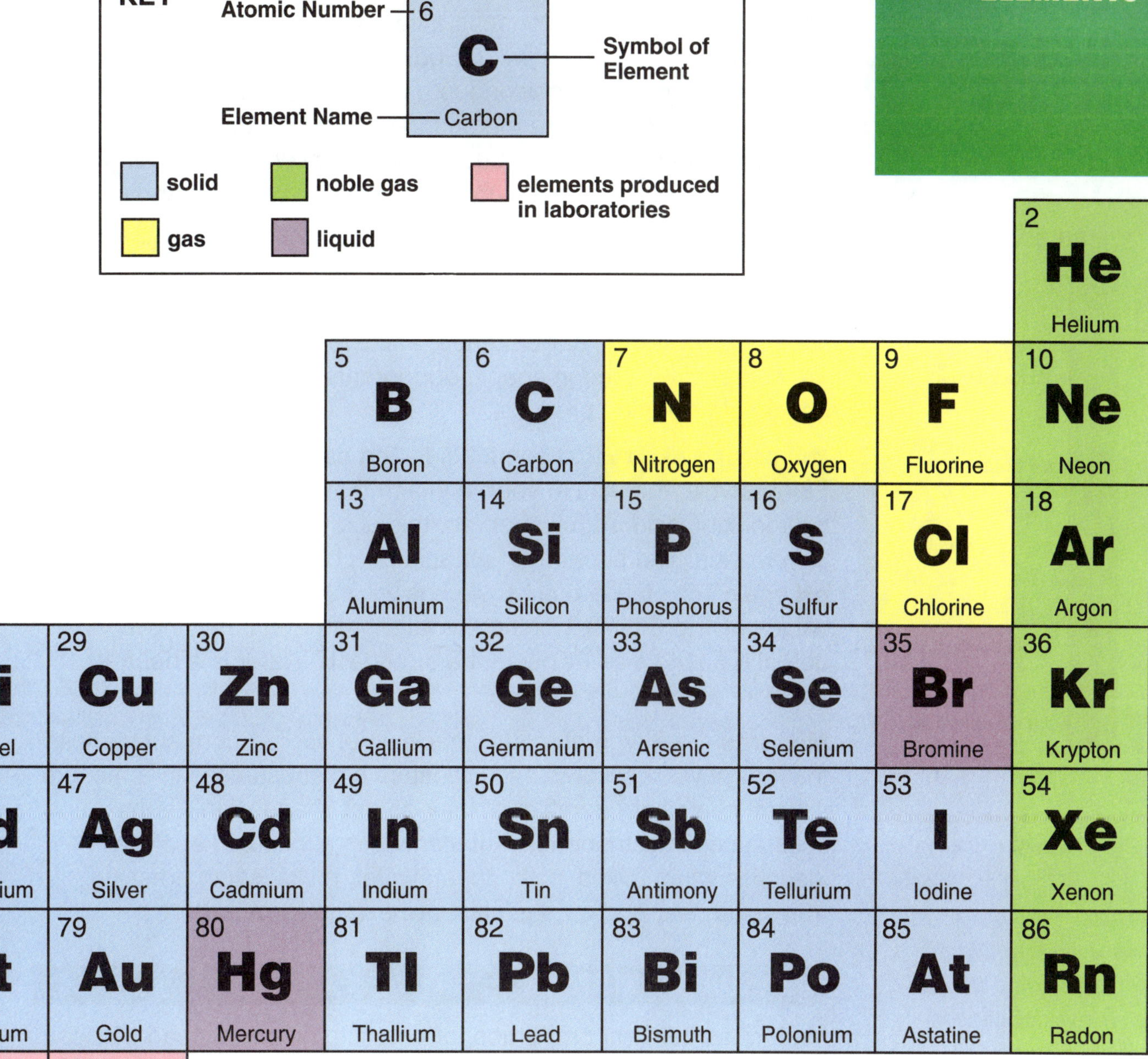

								2 He Helium
			5 B Boron	6 C Carbon	7 N Nitrogen	8 O Oxygen	9 F Fluorine	10 Ne Neon
			13 Al Aluminum	14 Si Silicon	15 P Phosphorus	16 S Sulfur	17 Cl Chlorine	18 Ar Argon
Ni ickel	29 Cu Copper	30 Zn Zinc	31 Ga Gallium	32 Ge Germanium	33 As Arsenic	34 Se Selenium	35 Br Bromine	36 Kr Krypton
d lladium	47 Ag Silver	48 Cd Cadmium	49 In Indium	50 Sn Tin	51 Sb Antimony	52 Te Tellurium	53 I Iodine	54 Xe Xenon
Pt atinum	79 Au Gold	80 Hg Mercury	81 Tl Thallium	82 Pb Lead	83 Bi Bismuth	84 Po Polonium	85 At Astatine	86 Rn Radon
un unnilium	111 Uuu Unununium							

Eu ropium	64 Gd Gadolinium	65 Tb Terbium	66 Dy Dysprosium	67 Ho Holmium	68 Er Erbium	69 Tm Thulium	70 Yb Ytterbium	71 Lu Lutetium
m ericium	96 Cm Curium	97 Bk Berkelium	98 Cf Californium	99 Es Einsteinium	100 Fm Fermium	101 Md Mendelevium	102 No Nobelium	103 Lr Lawrencium

ELEMENTS MEASURING MATTER

Compounds are substances composed of two or more elements that are chemically combined. Compounds are made of **molecules**. A molecule is a combination of two or more atoms. The properties of a compound are far different from the elements that make it up. For example, sodium chloride is a compound made up of the elements sodium and chlorine. Sodium is a poisonous white solid; chlorine is a greenish, poisonous gas. Yet when these elements are combined they create the substance sodium chloride, which is a harmless white crystalline substance we know as table salt! Water, another compound, is made up of two gases—hydrogen and oxygen.

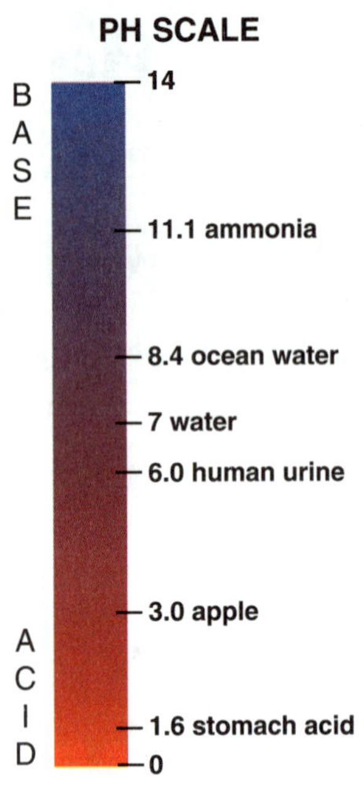

There are millions of different compounds. **Acids** and **bases** are among the most familiar and important groups of compounds. Acids are found in vinegar, aspirin, citrus fruits, some kinds of vegetables, soda pop, fertilizers, car batteries, and even your stomach! Bases are compounds used in soaps, deodorants, antacids, and certain household cleaning products.

You probably know that some acids and bases can be dangerous. For example, the acid in your stomach that helps you digest food is hydrochloric acid. At full strength, this acid can cause painful burns to your skin! The strength of an acid or a base is measured on a **pH scale**.The standard pH scale has values from 0 to14. Acids have values of 1 to 6 (with 1 being the strongest) and bases have values of 8 to 14 (with 14 being the strongest). Water is a neutral solution, and it has a value of 7.

Mixtures are a type of matter made up of two or more substances that are physically combined. Because the substances in a mixture are not chemically combined, they do not change. Unlike the substances in compounds, substances in a mixture keep their identities when mixed. Milk, ocean water, rocks, salad dressing, fruit salad, tea, and orange juice are examples of mixtures.

Milk is a mixture whose main component is water. Milk also contains fat and a weak acid called lactic acid. Ocean water is a mixture of water and various compounds, most of which are salts. The most common salt in ocean water is sodium chloride. Rocks are mixtures of minerals. The igneous rock granite is made of quartz, feldspar, and mica. Italian salad dressing is a mixture containing oil, vinegar, water, sugar, and spices.

MEASURING MATTER

Matter has different properties, or characteristics, that can be used to describe it. Color, odor, texture, shape, and state are examples of specific properties that can be used to describe a sample of matter. General properties of matter include mass, gravity, weight, volume, density, and temperature. These can be measured.

Mass is the amount of matter in an object. The mass of an object does not change unless you add matter to the object or take some matter away. Mass is measured in grams, kilograms, and other metric mass units. **Gravity** is a force of attraction between every object in the universe and every other object in the universe. The force of gravity between two objects depends on the masses of the two objects and the distance between them.

Weight is the measure of the force of gravity on an object. It is usually measured with a spring scale. The metric unit of weight is the **newton** (N), which is equivalent to about 2.2 pounds. Outside the lab, however, it is generally acceptable to measure weight in pounds and ounces, or their metric equivalents.

Mass and weight are not the same, but they are related. The more matter an object contains, the greater its weight. Because it is a measure of gravitational force, weight varies. A person weighing 120 pounds (54 kg) on Earth would weigh only 20 pounds (9 kg) on the moon! The same person would weigh almost 293 pounds (131.85 kg) on Jupiter, but only 48 pounds (21.6 kg) on Mars! But no matter where this person is in the universe, he or she will always have the same mass.

Volume is the amount of space occupied by an object. The volume of a solid with a regular shape, such as a cube, can be computed by multiplying the length of one side by itself three times. The volume of a liquid or an irregularly shaped solid can be found using a laboratory device called a graduated cylinder. Volume is measured in cubic inches, cubic centimeters, and larger and smaller units of length. Liquid volume is often measured in liters or gallons, and their smaller and larger equivalents.

Density is the mass per unit volume of a substance. Density is calculated by dividing the mass of a substance by its volume ($D=m \div v$).

Temperature is a measure of how fast the atoms in an object actually move. As the atoms speed up, an object's temperature increases. As the atoms slow down, an object's temperature decreases. Temperature is measured with a thermometer in either degrees Fahrenheit or degrees Celsius.

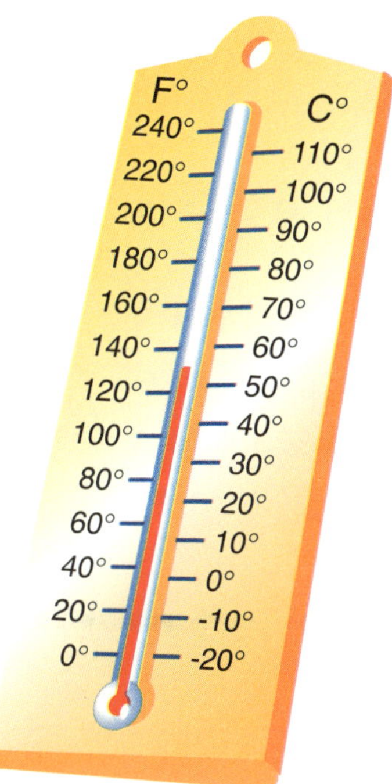

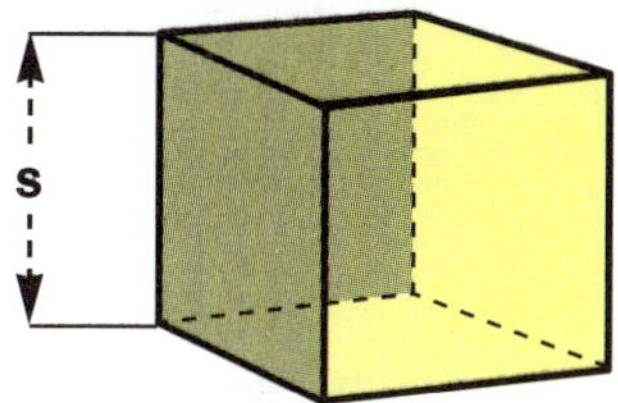

To find the volume (V) of a cube, multiply the length of one side (s) by itself three times.

$$s^3 = V$$

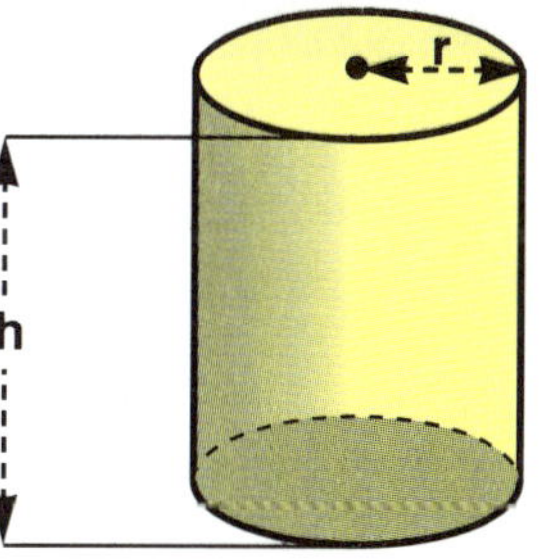

Calculate the volume (V) of a cylinder by multiplying the area of the base (b) by the height (h). Since the base of a cylinder is a circle, use the formula πr^2 to find the area.

$$\text{area of } b \times h = V$$

or

$$\pi r^2 \times h = V$$

MEASURING MATTER

How many centimeters are in an inch? How many liters are in a quart? How many pounds does a 7 kg bowling ball weigh? Metric and English measurements can easily be converted using the information in the table shown here.

If you enter a ten kilometer bicycle race, how many miles will you have to ride? Write your answer on paper.

ENGLISH AND METRIC CONVERSION CHART

To Change:	Multiply by:
Inches to Centimeters	2.54
Centimeters to Inches	0.39
Feet to Meters	0.30
Meters to Feet	3.28
Yards to Meters	0.91
Meters to Yards	1.09
Miles to Kilometers	1.61
Kilometers to Miles	0.62
Ounces to Grams	28.35
Grams to Ounces	0.035
Pounds to Kilograms	0.45
Kilograms to Pounds	2.21
Liters to Quarts	1.06
Liters to Gallons	0.26
Gallons to Liters	3.79
Square Inches to Square Centimeters	6.45
Square Centimeters to Square Inches	0.16
Square Feet to Square Meters	0.09
Square Meters to Square Feet	10.76
Square Miles to Square Kilometers	2.60
Square Kilometers to Square Miles	0.39

On paper, calculate your weight in kilograms and your height in centimeters.

CHAPTER 10

Light and Sound

WAVES
ELECTROMAGNETIC SPECTRUM

WAVES

Crashing surf, X rays, radio transmissions, light, sound, and microwaves are different types of waves. A **wave** is a motion that transfers energy from one place to another. **Energy** is the ability to do work. An object has energy either because it is in motion, or because energy is stored as a result of the object's condition or position. **Kinetic energy** is energy due to motion. **Potential energy** is stored energy.

All waves have two parts. The top of a wave is called the **crest**. The bottom, or valley, is the **trough**. **Wavelength** is the distance between a point on one wave and the identical point on the next wave. Wavelength can be measured from crest to crest, trough to trough, or anyplace in between. **Amplitude** is the greatest distance between the position of rest and the highest position on a wave.

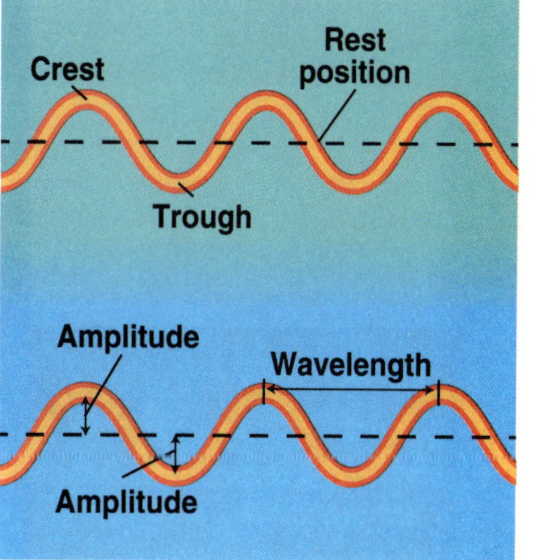

The **velocity** of a wave is the distance traveled by a single point on the wave in one second. Velocity is measured in units of length per second. Wave **frequency** is the number of waves that pass a given point in one second. Frequency is measured in a unit called **hertz**. One hertz equals one wave passing a given point in one second. The expression below shows how wavelength and frequency are related.

$$\text{velocity} = \text{wavelength} \times \text{frequency}$$

If velocity remains constant, waves with long wavelengths have low frequencies. Waves with short wavelengths have high frequencies.

ELECTROMAGNETIC SPECTRUM

The **electromagnetic spectrum** includes waves that are produced by the motion of electrically charged particles. Radio waves, infrared waves, light, ultraviolet rays, X rays, and gamma rays make up the electromagnetic spectrum. The spectrum consists of waves with a wide variety of wavelengths, but all electromagnetic waves travel at the same speed. This is called the speed of light. The speed of light in a vacuum is equal to 186,282 miles (299,792 kilometers) per second. **Radio waves** are used to cook foods in microwave ovens,

ELECTROMAGNETIC SPECTRUM

to transmit radio and television shows, and to operate cellular and cordless phones. **Infrared waves** from the sun warm the earth. These waves are also used to help detect tumors and areas of poor circulation in the body and to keep foods warm in restaurant kitchens. Special lenses collect infrared rays and make it possible to see people and other warm objects in complete darkness. **Ultraviolet (UV) rays** from the sun help to keep our planet warm. Too much UV radiation, however, causes skin cancer. UV lamps are used in medical facilities to kill bacteria and viruses and to sterilize instruments. Ultraviolet rays are also used to kill harmful microorganisms on certain foods. **X rays** and **gamma rays** are used mostly in medicine. X rays can detect broken bones and dental cavities. Gamma rays, which are given off by the chemical element radium, are used to treat some kinds of cancer.

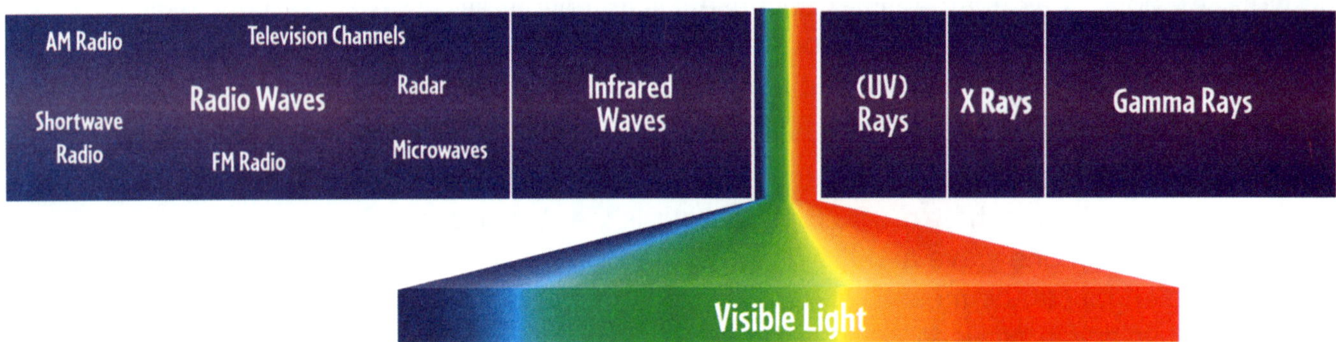

The frequency of middle C on a piano is 262 hertz. How many times per second does this sound vibrate? Write your answer on paper.

Light is the only visible part of the electromagnetic spectrum. Different types of matter transmit, reflect, or absorb light differently. **Transparent** matter transmits light, or allows light to pass completely through it. **Translucent** matter transmits light but scatters it, preventing you from being able to see things clearly. **Opaque** matter absorbs all light.

Visible light is a small part of the electromagnetic spectrum, but it also has a spectrum all its own called the **visible spectrum**. It may be difficult to believe, but white light is made up of all the colors of the rainbow—red, orange, yellow, green, blue, indigo, and violet.

Where have X rays been proven useful tools? Write your answer on paper.

You see color because of chemical reactions between light rays and your eyes. But why does an apple appear red and grass green? When white light, such as sunlight, strikes an object, the object **reflects**, or throws back, certain colors of the visible spectrum and **absorbs**, or takes in, the rest. An apple reflects red light waves but absorbs all of the other visible light waves. Grass reflects green light. White objects reflect all colors of the visible spectrum.

A mirror is a shiny surface that reflects most of the light that strikes it. When you look in a mirror, the image you see is light reflecting from you to the mirror and back. But the image is reversed. Hold up your right hand and your image appears to be holding up your left hand. There are various kinds of mirrors. Plane mirrors are flat mirrors that have a reflective coating of silver or aluminum on the front or back of the mirror. The image produced by a plane mirror is upright and true to size, but the image is reversed. Concave mirrors are curved inward. They are shaped like the bowl of a spoon. The image produced with a concave mirror is enlarged and inverted. A magnifying mirror is a surface that produces an image that is upright and enlarged. Convex mirrors curve outward and are shaped like the back of a spoon. Convex mirrors form images that are upright but smaller than the object producing the image.

Lenses are transparent objects that have at least one curved surface. They **refract**, or bend, light waves. Convex lenses are lenses that are thicker in the middle than they are along their edges. Certain camera lenses and magnifying glasses are convex lenses. Farsightedness can be corrected by glasses or contact lenses that are convex. Concave lenses are thin in the middle and thicker along their edges. Concave lenses are used in cameras, telescopes, eyeglasses, and contact lenses to correct nearsighted vision.

List some examples of transparent, translucent, and opaque items you might find in your kitchen. Write your answers on paper.

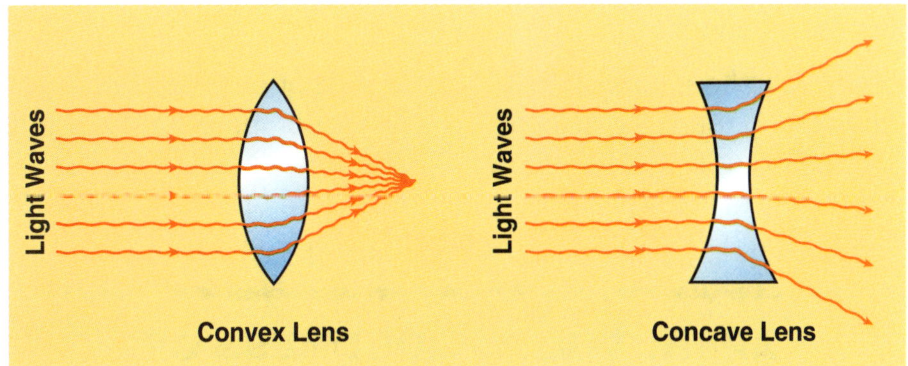

What type of lens is used to correct farsighted vision? Write your answer on paper.

LASERS

A **laser** is a beam of light that has one or, at most, several frequencies. Unlike visible light, a beam of laser light does not spread out, since all the waves travel in one narrow, focused direction. In certain types of surgery, lasers are used to make clean cuts through body tissues. The energy from the beam seals off blood vessels to reduce bleeding. Lasers are also used in compact disc (CD) players to maintain high-quality sound. Optical fibers in the communications industry use laser beams to carry communication signals. Lasers are also used to produce **holograms**, which are three-dimensional images that appear to float in space.

List some instruments that use lenses and mirrors to produce images. Write your answers on paper.

SOUND

SOUND

Sounds are produced when objects vibrate. Sound, like light, travels as waves. Unlike light waves, however, sound waves need a **medium**, or substance, through which to travel to conduct them. Air is the most common medium through which sound waves travel.

Do sounds travel fastest in solids, liquids, or gases? Write your answer on paper.

SOME MATERIALS THAT CONDUCT SOUND

Material	Speed of Sound (at 20°C)
Air	1,128 feet (344 meters) per second
Water	4,799 feet (1,463 meters) per second
Iron	16,826 feet (5,130 meters) per second
Copper	11,677 feet (3,560 meters) per second
Gold	5,717 feet (1,743 meters) per second

The speed of sound waves varies depending on the material through which the sound waves travel. The speed of sound also depends on the temperature of the medium. As the temperature rises, the speed of sound increases.

The denser a medium is, the faster sound will travel through it.

Humans can hear sounds as soft as a whisper or as loud as a jet plane getting ready for takeoff. The intensity of the sound depends on the amplitude of the sound waves. **Loudness** is a person's response to how strong a sound seems to him or her. Loudness is measured in a unit called the **decibel**, which is abbreviated dB.

APPROXIMATE LOUDNESS OF COMMON SOUNDS

Sound	Loudness	Sound	Loudness
Whisper	20 dB	Vacuum cleaner	80 dB
Rustling leaves	20 dB	Rock music	110 dB
Waves on a seashore	40 dB	Jet plane taking off	140 dB
Two people talking	60 dB		

Ultrasounds are sounds with frequencies greater than 20,000 hertz. Ultrasounds can't be heard, but they are very useful in medicine. Can you list a few of the uses of ultrasounds in medicine? Write your answers on paper.

Electrifying!

ELECTRICITY

Electricity is a form of energy associated with the movement of electrons—the negatively charged particles that orbit the nucleus of an atom. **Static electricity** is the buildup of positive or negative electrical charges on an object. You have probably observed static electricity if you've ever seen fabrics cling together after being taken out of a clothes dryer. As the fabrics rub together in the dryer, electrons are removed from some fabrics and become attached to other fabrics. The fabrics that lose electrons become positively charged, while the fabrics that gain electrons become negatively charged. The oppositely charged fabrics will attract each other and stick together.

The flow of electrons through a conductor, usually a metal substance, is called **electric current**. A measure of the strength needed to push electrons is called **voltage**. The energy of the electrons moving through a conductor can be used to do work, such as turning an electric motor. Electrical energy can also be changed to other forms of energy, such as light from a bulb or heat from a stove.

Some materials conduct electric current better than others. **Resistance** is the tendency of a material to oppose the flow of electrons. A **conductor** is a material that allows electrons to move easily through it. Metals are very good conductors of electricity. An **insulator** is a material that doesn't allow electrons to flow easily through it. Wood, plastic, rubber, foam, dry air, and glass are insulators.

A **circuit** is the path electrons follow as they flow through a conductor. In a **series circuit**, the current can travel along only one path. The amount of electric current traveling through a series circuit is the same in every part of the circuit. Many strings of holiday lights are wired as series circuits. If one bulb goes out, they all go out. **Parallel circuits** have separate paths through which electric current moves. Houses and other buildings are wired with parallel circuits.

Lightning is probably the most dramatic example of a discharge of static electricity. During a thunderstorm, negative charges build up on cloud bases and positive charges build up on the ground. When the potential difference between the two surfaces becomes great enough, a giant spark—lightning—travels between the cloud and the ground.

Direct current, or DC, flows only in one direction. Batteries provide direct current. Portable tape players, remote control devices, cameras, electric toys, and flashlights use DC. **Alternating current**, or AC, reverses its direction in a regular manner. Most lights and household appliances use AC. Devices such as portable stereos can operate on either current.

MAGNETISM

Magnetism is a force of attraction produced by an arrangement of electrons. The forces of attraction and repulsion are strongest near the **poles**, or ends, of a magnet. All magnets except circular magnets have two poles: a north pole and a south pole. Like poles repel one another. Unlike poles attract one another.

An electric current flowing through a conductor sets up a magnetic field. If the current is passed through a wire coiled around a piece of iron, the iron becomes a strong, temporary magnet. This magnet is called an **electromagnet**. Electromagnets are found in many devices, including stereo loudspeakers, doorbells, and certain types of construction equipment. This kind of magnet is magnetized only when electric current is flowing through it.

Generators in power plants produce most of the electricity you use every day. A **generator** is a device that produces an electric current by rotating loops of wire in a magnetic field. A generator gets its energy from a **turbine**, which is a large bladed wheel that spins very rapidly. The energy to turn the turbine comes from steam, moving water, or wind moving over its blades. Electrical energy produced in the generators is sent to a **step-up transformer**, which increases the voltage of the alternating current. The current leaves the transformer and travels through high-voltage wires to your neighborhood. There it is sent to a **step-down transformer** that reduces the voltage to a safe level before the current moves into your home.

The region around a magnet where magnetic forces act is called a magnetic field. Magnetic fields are invisible. The force lines they produce, however, can be modeled when iron slivers are sprinkled around bar magnets, as shown in the diagrams.

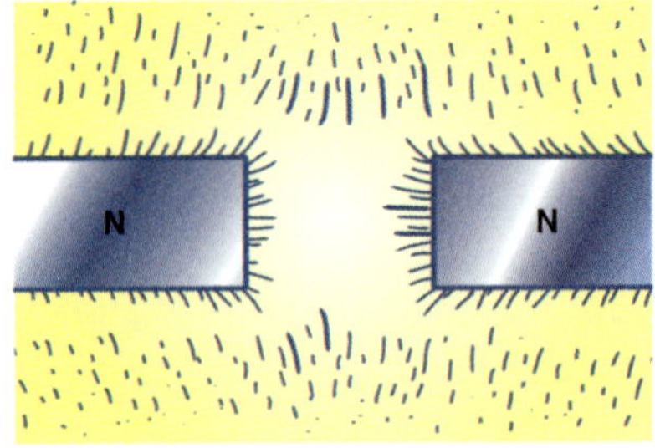

magnetic fields of like poles repel

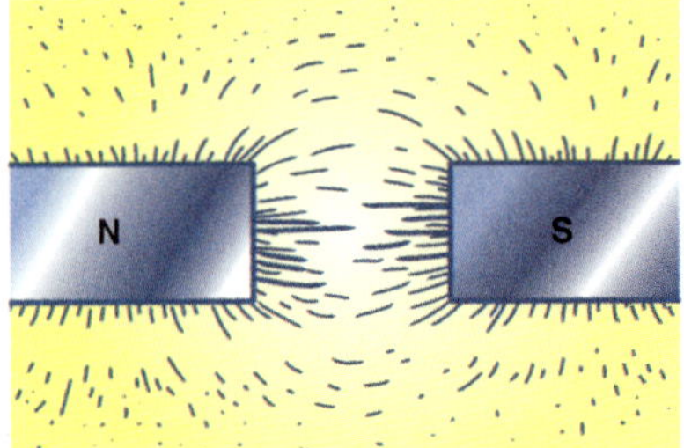

magnetic fields of unlike poles attract

SUPERCONDUCTIVITY

Superconductors are materials that have no electrical resistance. This means that an electric current can flow through such materials indefinitely without losing energy. When combined with magnetic fields, superconductors allow things to levitate, or float in midair! Experimental trains in Japan glide smoothly a few inches above their tracks without touching them! Powerful magnets below the train cars and rails made of superconducting materials permit the trains to remain above the rails. Such trains are extremely energy-efficient and don't pollute the environment as much as conventional means of transportation do.

CHAPTER 12

Forces and Motion

FORCES

A **force** is a cause of motion or change to an object. When two objects exert forces on each other that are equal in strength and opposite in direction, the two forces are **balanced**. For example, if each team in a tug-of-war pulls with the same amount of force, nobody moves because the forces exerted by each team are balanced. However, if one team exerts more force on the rope than the other team, members of the other team are pulled forward because the forces are **unbalanced**.

Wearing leather-soled shoes on an icy sidewalk is unsafe. What kind of soles might decrease your chances of falling? Write your answer on paper.

Friction is another familiar force. Friction opposes motion between two surfaces that are in contact with each other. It is this force that allows you to walk along the ground, catch a ball, or hold a flower between your fingers. The amount of friction depends on two things—the types of surfaces that are in contact and the size of the forces pressing the surfaces together. The size of force is determined by measuring the mass and acceleration of each object.

When you go swimming, you may have noticed that your body feels lighter in water than it does in air. You may even be able to float in water. That's because water pushes up on your body. **Buoyancy** is an upward force exerted on an object by a fluid—a liquid or a gas—in which the object is immersed. You might think that buoyancy depends on the weight of the object immersed in the fluid. If this were the case, heavy objects would sink and light objects would float. This is not necessarily true! A 10-pound (4.5-kg) log will float in water, while most rocks of the same weight will sink. The property that determines whether an object will sink or float is density. Recall from page 49 that density is mass per unit volume. An object having a density greater than that of a fluid will sink in that fluid. An object with a density less than the density of a fluid will float in that fluid.

NEWTON'S LAWS OF MOTION
WORK AND MACHINES

List some objects that will float in water. Write your answers on paper.

NEWTON'S LAWS OF MOTION

In the late 1600s, a scientist named Isaac Newton observed that forces can change the motion of an object. From his observations, Newton formulated three laws of motion.

NEWTON'S THREE LAWS OF MOTION

Newton's First Law of Motion

An object in motion stays in motion unless it is acted upon by an outside force. Likewise, an object at rest will stay at rest unless an unbalanced force acts upon it. This tendency of an object to remain in motion or at rest is called **inertia**.

Newton's Second Law of Motion

A net force can change the speed, the direction, or the speed and direction of an object. Changes in the speed and/or direction of the object depend on the size of the force and the mass of the object. Newton's second law of motion can be expressed mathematically as shown in the equation below.

Force = mass x acceleration

Acceleration is the rate of change of an object's speed and direction.

Newton's Third Law of Motion

For every action, there is an opposite and equal reaction. In other words, when one object exerts a force on a second object, the second object exerts a force on the first that is equal in size and opposite in direction.

WORK AND MACHINES

To a scientist, **work** is done when a force is used to move an object for a distance against some form of resistance. For example, if you push or pull an object, and that object moves in the direction of the force, work is done.

A **machine** is a device that replaces human or animal efforts and makes work easier. A **simple machine** makes work easier by changing the size or direction of a force. **Compound machines** are devices made up of more than one simple machine.

There are six types of simple machines: the pulley, the wheel and axle, the lever, the inclined plane, the screw, and the wedge.

To do work, you exert a force, or an effort, to move something that resists being moved, called a **resistance**. When using a machine to do work, the force you apply to the machine is called the **effort force**. The force exerted by the machine on the object being moved is called the **resistance force**. The **mechanical advantage** of the machine is the ratio of the effort force to the resistance force.

Pulleys are simple machines that can be used to change the direction of a force or to reduce the effort force needed to move an object. A fixed pulley changes the direction of the effort force. A movable pulley reduces the effort force. A block and tackle is a combination of fixed and movable pulleys that allows a person to lift very heavy objects.

Doorknobs, faucet handles, and bicycle gears are examples of the simple machine called the **wheel and axle**. A wheel and axle consists of two wheels of different diameters that rotate together. With a wheel and axle, the effort is usually applied to the wheel having the greater diameter. The resistance is exerted by the smaller wheel, or the axle.

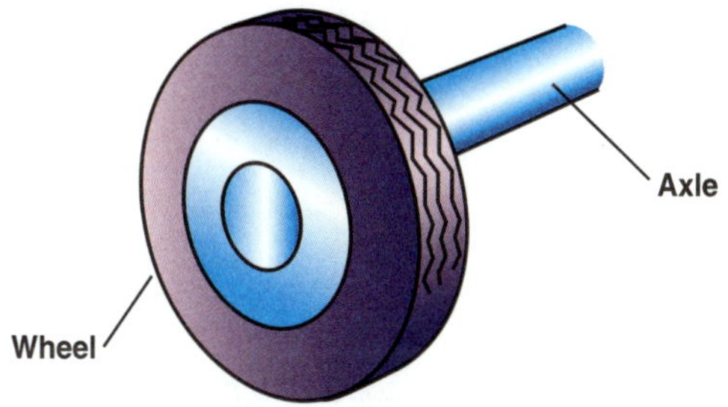

A **lever** is a bar that is free to turn about a fixed point, or **fulcrum**. The part of the lever to which the effort force is applied is the **effort arm**. The part of the lever that exerts the resistance force is the **resistance arm**. There are three kinds of levers. In a first-class lever, the fulcrum is between the effort arm and the resistance arm. Scissors and pry bars are examples of first-class levers. In a second-class lever, the resistance is located between the effort force and the fulcrum. A nutcracker and a wheelbarrow are examples of second-class levers. In a third-class lever, the effort force is located between the resistance force and the fulcrum. A baseball bat and a broomstick are examples of third-class levers.

An **inclined plane** is a sloping surface used to raise or lower objects. A ramp is an example of an inclined plane. A **screw** is an inclined plane wrapped in a spiral around a cylinder. The threads of a screw form a ramp that runs from the tip of the screw to its top. As a screw is driven into a board, the wood moves along the threads. A **wedge** is an inclined plane with one or two sloping sides. Like a screw, a wedge is a moving inclined plane. Knives, ax blades, and chisels are wedges.

The formula for finding out how much work is done is shown below.

W = F x D
Work = amount of Force applied times the Distance an object is moved

To understand mechanical advantage, think of a crowbar and a fulcrum. If the crowbar is placed under a load, and the distance from the load to the fulcrum is about one-third the distance from the fulcrum to the crowbar handle, the mechanical advantage is 3. The ratio of the effort force (the force you apply to the crowbar) to the resistance force (the force exerted by the crowbar to move the load) is 3 to 1.

Which of Newton's laws best explains how a rocket takes off?

SCIENCE EXPERIMENTS

Scientists perform experiments to find out information and to test theories. There are three basic parts to every experiment: the hypothesis, the experiment, and the conclusion. When doing an experiment for school, use the following format.

THE HYPOTHESIS

A hypothesis is an educated guess or prediction about the experiment that you are going to perform. What do you think the outcome of the experiment will be? Write your hypothesis as one sentence.

THE EXPERIMENT

There are three parts to an experiment: the materials, the procedure, and the results.

Materials: Write a list of the materials you need for the experiment. Be sure to specify exact amounts. Then gather all the materials before you begin.

Procedure: List all of the steps you must follow to perform the actual experiment. Number each step in order. Then, perform the experiment. (Sometimes mistakes are made or you don't achieve the desired results. If this happens, redo the experiment from the beginning.)

Results: Record the outcome or results of the experiment. They may be written as a list, chart, or graph.

THE CONCLUSION

Compare the results of the experiment to the hypothesis. Decide whether the hypothesis was correct or incorrect. Perform the experiment several times to test the validity of your results. Write a brief statement explaining why the experiment proves or disproves the hypothesis. Share the results with other people.

INDEX

INDEX

ANSWER KEY

PAGE 6
Because they don't have all the characteristics of organisms, viruses by themselves are not living things.

PAGE 7
All are used for movement: flagella are whiplike structures, cilia are short hairlike features, and pseudopods are fingerlike extensions.

PAGE 8
Penicillin

PAGE 10
Carrots, radishes, turnips, and beets are a few edible roots.

PAGE 11
Tomatoes and cucumbers are two fruits often found in salads; no—they are both vegetables

PAGE 14
1. Both processes occur in cells. Photosynthesis takes place only in plants. Respiration takes place in all living things. During photosynthesis, energy is stored. During respiration, energy is released. The starting products of photosynthesis are the end products of respiration, and vice versa.
2. Humans are primary consumers when they eat plants. Humans are secondary consumers when they eat animals that have eaten plants.

PAGE 15
cell wall and chloroplasts

PAGE 20
reptiles

PAGE 25
1. magnetite; graphite
2. Examples of igneous rocks are granite, basalt, obsidian, and pumice. Examples of sedimentary rocks are shale, sandstone, chalk, coal, and limestone. Examples of metamorphic rocks are gneiss, marble, slate, and schist.

PAGE 26
a pterodactyl, an extinct type of flying reptile

PAGE 30
1. 77˚ F
2. At the time and place of the report, the air is holding only 60% of the water vapor it is capable of holding.

PAGE 36
the North American plate

PAGE 37
inner core, outer core, mantle, crust; 7,984 miles (12,854 kilometers)

PAGE 38
bombs, cinders, ash

PAGE 40
spring tides, because the gravitational forces of the sun, moon, and Earth are combined

PAGE 41
December

PAGE 45
Answers will vary. Possible answers include: water vapor condensing on a bathroom mirror after a hot shower; an ice cube melting in a glass of water; a puddle evaporating on a sunny day.

PAGE 50
1. 6.2 miles
2. your weight in pounds x .45; your height in inches x 2.54

PAGE 52
1. 262 times per second
2. Answers will vary. Possible answers include: airports, government buildings, and hospitals.

PAGE 53
1. Answers will vary. Possible answers include: transparent—window glass, many drinking glasses, and glass baking dishes; translucent—waxed paper; opaque—metal cookie sheets and aluminum foil.
2. convex lenses
3. Answers will vary. Possible answers include: cameras, telescopes, and microscopes.

PAGE 54
1. solids
2. Answers will vary. Possible answers include: imaging the heart, thyroid, liver; and checking the development of a fetus before it is born.

PAGE 57
thick rubber soles

PAGE 58
Answers will vary. Possible answers include: a block of wood, a leaf, a foam ball, a rubber raft.

PAGE 59
the third law